GILGAMESH

GILGAMESH

A New Verse Rendering by
STANLEY LOMBARDO

Introduction by
GARY BECKMAN

Hackett Publishing Company, Inc.
Indianapolis/Cambridge

22 21 20 19   1 2 3 4 5 6 7

For further information, please address
Hackett Publishing Company, Inc.
P.O. Box 44937
Indianapolis, Indiana 46244-0937

www.hackettpublishing.com

Cover design by Brian Rak
Interior design by Laura Clark
Composition by Aptara, Inc.

Library of Congress Cataloging-in-Publication Data

Names: Lombardo, Stanley, 1943– translator. | Beckman, Gary M.,
  writer of introduction.
Title: Gilgamesh / translated by Stanley Lombardo ; introduction by
  Gary Beckman.
Other titles: Gilgamesh. English.
Description: Indianapolis : Hackett Publishing Company, Inc., [2019] |
  Includes bibliographical references.
Identifiers: LCCN 2018036034 | ISBN 9781624667732 (cloth) |
  ISBN 9781624667725 (pbk.)
Subjects: LCSH: Epic poetry, Assyro-Babylonian.
Classification: LCC PJ3771.G5 E5 2019 | DDC 892/.1—dc23
LC record available at https://lccn.loc.gov/2018036034

CONTENTS

INTRODUCTION

The hero Gilgamesh was well known throughout the Near East during the first millennium BCE. In addition to the copies of his adventures included in the libraries of Assyrian and Babylonian scholars and kings, many prosperous men proudly carried personal (cylinder) seals depicting the battle of Gilgamesh and his faithful companion Enkidu with the monstrous Bull of Heaven. Outside of his Mesopotamian homeland, references to Gilgamesh appear in the Aramaic-language *Book of Giants* preserved among the Dead Sea Scrolls of Qumran in Palestine (second century BCE) and a bit later in the tract *On the Nature of Animals* by the Greek writer Aelian (second century CE). Nonetheless, with the eclipse of the Mesopotamian literary tradition by that of Greece and Rome, completed by the first century of the Common Era, Gilgamesh had largely been forgotten until the rediscovery of the cultures of ancient Assyria and Babylonia less than 200 years ago.

The Rediscovery of Mesopotamia and Its Culture

The mid-nineteenth century CE witnessed the beginnings of a new stage of the rivalry between France and England to establish expansive empires and to extend their political and cultural influence throughout the world. In the declining Ottoman Empire, which in this period still included Mesopotamia (modern Iraq and northern Syria), the pioneers of European imperialism were the British and French diplomats stationed in the Sultan's provincial capitals. Among these men were the French consul Paul-Émile Botta (1802–1870), who served in Mosul (in the north of today's Iraq). In addition to his regular duties, Botta began to investigate the nearby artificial mounds ("tells") that turned out to contain the ruins of the capital cities of ancient Assyria. From 1842 to 1844 he dug at Khorsabad, uncovering the remains of ancient Dur-Sharrukin, "Fortress of Sargon," the royal city of Sargon II (722–705 BCE), a ruler of Assyria mentioned in the Hebrew Bible.

The renown accruing to the French "proto-archaeologist" prompted the British to dispatch their own Austen Henry Layard (1817–1894) to Mosul, who from 1845 through 1847 excavated the giant mound of Küyünjik, situated directly across the Tigris River from the Ottoman provincial center. Here he found what had once been the famous city of Nineveh, whose destruction was foretold in the biblical books of Nahum and Zephaniah. Perhaps Layard's most important discovery at Nineveh was the library of the last significant king of Assyria, Ashurbanipal (668–ca. 627 BCE); the contents of thousands of clay tablets and fragments were packed up and shipped to the British Museum in London.

The excavations of Botta and Layard, although clumsy and destructive by today's archaeological standards, marked the beginning of the study of ancient Mesopotamia and the surrounding nations whose civilizations developed under its influence.

The Cuneiform Writing System

The Assyrian documents dispatched to London constituted the first substantial body of material inscribed in the cuneiform script that became available for investigation by Western scholars, and therefore the entire enterprise of studying ancient records on clay has been called "Assyriology" up to the present day, even if only a portion of the relevant material was in fact produced in Assyria.

It is important to note that cuneiform (Neo-Latin "wedge-shaped" [script]) is a writing system and not a language. Invented in the closing centuries of the fourth millennium BCE in southern Mesopotamia to keep records in Sumerian, by ca. 2600 BCE cuneiform had been adapted to express the Semitic Akkadian language, whose major later northern and southern dialects were Assyrian and Babylonian, respectively. But cuneiform was also borrowed to write non-Mesopotamian tongues completely unrelated to either Sumerian or Akkadian—or indeed to one another. These included the Indo–European languages of ancient Anatolia (modern Turkey), most prominently Hittite, as well as Elamite at home in southwestern Iran and Hurrian in northern Syria and easternmost Anatolia. This situation might well be compared to the use today of the Latin alphabetic script, with appropriate modification, to express languages as different as English, Turkish, and Vietnamese.

But whereas the Latin script has been in continuous use since its invention ca. 550 BCE, in the 1840s no one had read a cuneiform text since the late first century CE. At least that is when the latest known (Babylonian) inscription in this type of writing was produced. Therefore, cuneiform had first to be deciphered to enable the recovery of the wealth of historical, economic, and cultural information preserved on the clay tablets. Several schoolteachers, university professors, and gentleman scholars, primarily from England, Ireland, France, and Germany, working independently, undertook this daunting task. The tablets Layard sent to London proved crucial in this process by providing sufficient material for thorough study. By 1857 cuneiform had been largely deciphered, as demonstrated by a test in which four of the leading students of the script were each presented with an Assyrian royal inscription previously unknown to them and then independently produced nearly identical English translations.

A few years later, the British Museum engaged a young apprentice banknote engraver and amateur cuneiform enthusiast, George Smith (1840–1876), to help sort and catalogue the innumerable tablet fragments held by that institution. During the course of his duties he kept up with progress in the decipherment of cuneiform, ultimately himself becoming an expert on the script. In 1872 he was startled to recognize striking parallels to the Biblical account of Noah's Flood in a mythological passage on a damaged Akkadian tablet. (We now realize that what Smith had found was an exemplar of Tablet XI of the version of the Gilgamesh Epic translated in this volume.) Smith's widely attended lecture concerning this discovery was a sensation, followed in 1876 by the publication of his *The Chaldean Account of Genesis*. In response to public enthusiasm for his seeming confirmation of the veracity of Christian scripture, Smith himself was sent out to Nineveh—first under the auspices of a popular newspaper and later under those of the British Museum itself—to search for further relevant material. On the third of these expeditions he was stricken with dysentery and died near Aleppo.

Nonetheless, other scholars have continued Smith's work on the reconstruction of the entire text of the Epic, with major (partial) editions appearing in 1884 and 1930. By the time of Andrew George's most recent comprehensive edition (2003), scholars had recovered around 2,450 of an estimated original 3,000 lines. Hopefully, with future excavation and discovery, we will eventually possess the entirety of the Epic, but we certainly already have the major portion and should expect no major textual surprises to challenge our philological and literary–critical interpretations.

Even in its incomplete form, the Epic has served as inspiration for artists from the nineteenth century to the present, providing the basis for numerous literary retellings, psychoanalytical explorations, and even operas. Poets have rendered it—some faithfully, some more loosely—into most modern languages. No other work from ancient Mesopotamian literature has enjoyed such popularity.

Gilgamesh and Noah

The excitement generated by Smith's 1872 discovery had little to do with the figure of Gilgamesh, but rather it centered on the report delivered to the hero in Tablet XI by his distant ancestor Utanapishtim, whose name means "He Who Found Life." To explain how he and his wife alone among humans had come to be granted immortality, the poet here provides Utanapishtim with a narrative that he has repurposed and adapted from a composition of the Old Babylonian period (ca. eighteenth–seventeenth centuries BCE), a text that Assyriologists refer to as "The Story of Atrahasis" after its main human character.[1]

This earlier composition covers a much larger slice of primeval history than its excerpt in the Gilgamesh Epic. It explains how humans were created in order to perform the labor that the junior gods had refused to do, how the ever-increasing numbers of people had disturbed the peace of their divine masters, and how the latter had decided to rectify the situation by eradicating human-ity. However, the single deity Ea, God of Wisdom, became the protector of humankind and advised his people on how to thwart the initial divine attempts at their annihilation. When the gods ultimately sought to destroy humanity by means of the Deluge and swore a solemn oath among themselves not to divulge this plan, Ea circumvented his promise by delivering his life-saving advice to Atrahasis ("Exceedingly Wise") through the reed wall of his home. From this point on, the narrative inserted into the Gilgamesh Epic closely parallels that of the Old Babylonian poem.

The degree of similarity between the stories of Utanapishtim and of Noah is well demonstrated in a comparison of their respective accounts of the after-math of the Great Flood. The Mesopotamian survivor relates his ordeal to Gilgamesh as follows:

> Six days and seven nights the gale-winds blew,
> The rain poured down, the Flood flattened the land.
> But when the seventh day dawned
> The winds died down, and the water subsided.
> The sea that had writhed like a woman in labor
> Now was calm, the storm over, the Deluge ended.
> I opened a window, and sunlight fell on my face.

---

1. The poet who adapted this older source for the Standard Babylonian Gilgamesh Epic neglected to change the name of the tale's protagonist from Atrahasis to Utanapishtim in Tablet XI, lines 45 and 189.

I looked at the weather, and it was perfectly calm,
But all of the people had turned into clay,
And the land was as flat as the roof of a house.
I sank to my knees and wept,
Tears running all down my face.
I scanned the ocean's horizon in all directions
And saw fourteen patches of land emerging.
The ship came to ground on Nimush Mountain,
Mount Nimush held it fast and did not let it move.
A first day and a second day Nimush Mountain
    held the boat fast and did not let it move.
A third day and a fourth day Nimush Mountain
    held the boat fast and did not let it move.
A fifth day and a sixth day Nimush Mountain
    held the boat fast and did not let it move.
When the seventh day dawned
I brought out a dove and let it go.
The dove flew off but then came back to me;
There was no place to land and so it came back.
I brought out a swallow and let it go.
The swallow flew off but then came back to me;
There was no place to land and so it came back.
I brought out a raven and let it go.
The raven flew off and saw the water subsiding.
It found food, cawed, and did not come back.
Then I sacrificed incense to the Four Winds,
Pouring out offerings on the mountain top.
I set out seven pots and another seven,
Piling beneath them cane, cedar, and myrtle.
The gods smelled the savor, smelled the sweet savor,
And gathered like flies around the sacrifice.

(Tablet XI 120–57)

The King James Bible describes the conclusion of Noah's tribulations thus:

4. And the ark rested in the seventh month, on the seventeenth day of the month, upon the mountains of Ararat. 5. And the waters decreased continually until the tenth month: in the tenth month, on the first day of the month, were the tops of the mountains seen.

6. And it came to pass at the end of forty days, that Noah opened the window of the ark which he had made: 7. And he sent forth a raven, which went forth to and fro, until the waters were dried up from off the earth. 8. Also he sent forth a dove from him, to see if the waters were abated from off the face of the ground; 9. But the dove found no rest for the sole of her foot, and she returned unto him into the ark, for the waters were on the face of the whole earth: then he put forth his hand, and took her, and pulled her in unto him into the ark. 10. And he stayed yet other seven days; and again he sent forth the dove out of the ark;

11. And the dove came in to him in the evening; and, lo, in her mouth was an olive leaf pluckt off: so Noah knew that the waters were abated from off the earth.

12. And he stayed yet other seven days; and sent forth the dove; which returned not again unto him any more. 13. And it came to pass in the six hundredth and first year, in the first month, the first day of the month, the waters were dried up from off the earth: and Noah removed the covering of the ark, and looked, and, behold, the face of the ground was dry. . . . 20. And Noah builded an altar unto the LORD; and took of every clean beast, and of every clean fowl, and offered burnt offerings on the altar. 21. And the LORD smelled a sweet savour; and the LORD said in his heart, I will not again curse the ground any more for man's sake; for the imagination of man's heart is evil from his youth; neither will I again smite any more every thing living, as I have done. (Genesis 4–14, 20–21)

Despite efforts to utilize these two accounts as evidence for an actual worldwide (or at least regional) catastrophe, there is no geological evidence for synchronous wide-ranging flooding over the entirety of the Near East, let alone the entire Earth. More significantly, the *narrative details* here—the exploration by means of birds, the coming to rest of the vessel upon particular mountains, the burnt offerings presented immediately upon disembarkation—indicate that the texts partake of a single *literary* tradition. The direction of borrowing is not in doubt: Since "The Story of Atrahasis" was inscribed hundreds of years prior to the earliest possible date for the composition of the Hebrew Bible, the tale must be of Mesopotamian origin. Most likely, intellectuals among the Judahites exiled to Babylonia in the sixth century BCE, some of whom learned cuneiform in order to serve in the local bureaucracy, adopted the story from their Babylonian "schoolbooks" or scribal colleagues.

A major difference between the Biblical and Akkadian accounts is the role the Deluge plays within the respective national traditions. In the Hebrew Bible, as an incident within the development of their relationship to God as set forth in the Torah, men bring their destruction upon themselves as a result of their wicked behavior. While after the trial God promises not to repeat the eliminationist flooding, he insists that human nature remains essentially evil.

In Mesopotamia by contrast—as seen more clearly in the fuller account provided in "The Story of Atrahasis"—there is no question of human disobedience or perversity involved. Humans in their multitudes and noisy, frenetic activity had simply become a nuisance within the once-serene universe, leading the gods to seek to eliminate them. But following the example of the Mother Goddess, they almost immediately regret their decision:

> Belet-ili cried out in her lovely voice,
> Our Lady wailing like a woman in childbirth:
> "The days of old have turned into clay
> Because I said bad things among the gods.
> How could I say bad things among the gods,
> Declare a war to destroy my people?
> I am the one who gave birth to these people,
> And now they fill the ocean like fish!"
> The Anunnaki wept along with her;
> Tears in their eyes, the gods were weeping;
> Their lips were dry and parched with fever.
>   (Tablet XI 109–19)

Indeed, it is their relief in learning of the survival of Utanapishtim, who immediately takes up his duties of caring for and feeding the gods, that leads them to bestow upon him and his spouse the eternal life that lies beyond the reach of all mortals.

The Human King Gilgamesh?

"The Sumerian King List," a text first attested in fragmentary form under the Third Dynasty of Ur (ca. 2112–2004 BCE), was a piece of propaganda claiming that—in conformity with the intention of the gods—rule over the entirety of Sumer (southernmost Mesopotamia) had always been held by a single city and its dynasty, before passing in succession to another polity. Historically this was untrue, for contemporary Sumerian-language royal inscriptions reveal that the region had long been home to a fair number of independent city-states, but the work served to justify the empire of the monarchs of Ur under whom it had apparently been composed. Its best preserved version dates to the very early second millennium BCE, when it had been adapted to buttress the claims to dominion of the city of Isin. Among the early rulers of the land listed here we find Bilgames—an earlier form of Gilgamesh—occupying the sixth place among the monarchs of the First Dynasty of Uruk (Early Dynastic Period; mid-third millennium BCE). But the historical existence of this figure is doubtful, if only due to the fantastic length of reign assigned to him—126 years. No records dating to his alleged reign have been recovered.

What is certain, however, is that a minor deity Bilgames is already mentioned in a text from the city of Shuruppak dating to around 2500 BCE and is the recipient of votive mace heads offered at about this time. The same figure was later held to be an ancestor of the rulers of the Ur III state. Indeed, it was almost certainly this spurious genealogical connection that prompted the composition—undoubtedly based on oral sources—by their court poets of the early Sumerian-language narratives featuring Bilgames/Gilgamesh.

The Sumerian Gilgamesh Tales

Five of these narratives have been recovered, primarily in copies from Babylonian scribal schools of the early second millennium BCE. (The titles are not ancient, but have been assigned by modern scholars.)

1) *Bilgames and Akka* relates how the king of Uruk and his servant Enkidu lead their city in successful resistance to oppressive demands made upon them by the ruler of the rival town of Kish.

2) *Bilgames and Huwawa,* preserved in two somewhat differing versions, recounts the journey of the hero and his retainer, here accompanied by troops from Uruk, to the Cedar Forest, where they slay its guardian and proceed to harvest timber.

3) In *Bilgames and the Bull of Heaven* the king rebuffs the sexual advances of Inanna/Ishtar and in response the goddess turns loose the fearsome beast upon Uruk. Bilgames and Enkidu battle and ultimately slaughter the rampaging bovine, further insulting the goddess by throwing one of its "haunches"—a euphemism for genitalia—in her face.

4) *Bilgames and the Nether World* tells of Enkidu's mission to recover some of his master's prized possessions from the subterranean realm of the dead. Cautioned by Bilgames to behave correctly and not to call attention to himself in Hades, Enkidu nonetheless disobeys these instructions and is consequently unable to return to the earth. Bilgames is bereft, but the sympathetic deities Enki and the Sun God Shamash arrange for Enkidu's ghost to visit briefly with him. The story concludes with Enkidu's first-hand description of the various sad lots of those confined to the underworld.

5) *The Death of Bilgames* opens with the hero lying in delirium on his deathbed, where he sees a vision of the gods in council, debating his fate. Despite his mixed divine–human parentage, they rule that he is mortal and must therefore die, but that in consolation he should be awarded the position of judge in the hereafter. Following a break in the text, preparations for the funeral and interment of the king are discussed, including a lengthy description of the gifts that he will take along with him for presentation to the officialdom of his new home.

Of these compositions only *Bilgames and Huwawa*, *Bilgames and the Bull of Heaven*, and *Bilgames and the Nether World* contributed directly to the Akkadian-language tradition, although elements of *The Death of Bilgames* were reworked to describe the funeral of Enkidu in the final version (Tablet VIII).

The Akkadian Gilgamesh Epic

From the Old Babylonian period (early second millennium BCE) come two well-preserved Akkadian-language tablets, now in collections at the University of Pennsylvania and at Yale University, that together deal with the meeting of Gilgamesh and Enkidu and their mooting of plans for an expedition to the Cedar Forest. Numerous more fragmentary tablets from various Mesopotamian sites dating to this era are also known, but they do not seem to be copies of a standardized text. The same is true of the material from the Late Bronze Age (later second millennium BCE), which in addition to Akkadian-language pieces also includes accounts in the Hittite and Hurrian tongues of the adventures of Gilgamesh. Furthermore, the Akkadian Gilgamesh tradition is represented for this era by finds from the periphery of the world that employed the cuneiform script—from Megiddo in Palestine, from Ugarit on the north Syrian coast, from Emar on the middle course of the Euphrates River, and most importantly from the Hittite capital Hattusa in central Anatolia.

The Standard Babylonian Gilgamesh Epic

The Standard Babylonian Epic translated in this volume—so called after the literary Akkadian (Babylonian) dialect in which it is written—is initially attested on tablets from Babylonia and Assyria dating to the first centuries of the first millennium BCE. By far the largest source of relevant manuscripts is the tablet collections of the Neo-Assyrian kings, particularly the library assembled on behalf of Ashurbanipal at his royal seat Nineveh (Küyünjik). Remarkably, whatever their find-spots, these tablets generally present a codified text differing at most only in orthography or "spelling"; the division into tablets is identical across the sources. Therefore, scholars also often refer to this composition as the Canonical Version.

Nonetheless, grammatical features of the Standard Babylonian Epic indicate that it had been composed several hundred years before the inscription of the recovered manuscripts. (This situation is rather like having access to the Middle English *Canterbury Tales* of Geoffrey Chaucer only through an original-language modern paperback edition.) A scribal exercise from Ugarit displaying great similarities to the opening lines of Tablet I of the canonical text shows that the epic had assumed more or less its final form by the middle of the thirteenth century BCE. The Mesopotamians credited this creation to one Sîn-lēqi-unninnī (whose name means "The Moon God Listens to My Prayer"), otherwise known only in Babylonian tradition as a sage advisor to an earlier ruler.

Although yet another name for the Standard Babylonian Epic is the Twelve Tablet Version, the reader will note that only eleven tablets have been rendered here. This is because most authorities recognize Tablet XII as an awkward appendix to the composition, probably added at a relatively late point in its development. It is a close prose translation of the Sumerian tale *Bilgames and the Nether World* mentioned above, whose details contradict what we read of the fate of Enkidu in Tablet VII and whose presence spoils the splendid symmetry of the frame narrative of Tablets I and XI centered on the walls of Uruk (see below).

Akkadian Epic Poetry

The meter of Akkadian epic poetry, as evidenced in the Standard Babylonian Gilgamesh Epic and other literary works such as the *Enuma Elish* (the so-called "Babylonian Creation Epic"), is based upon patterns of syntactic units rather than of syllabic stress, so it cannot be rendered authentically in English verse, which depends upon the latter. The translator compensates where possible by crafting lines with two main stresses flanking a central syntactic pause. To aid the modern reader, he has also formatted the text into paragraphs rather than retaining the couplets and quatrains of the original.

Even after this modification, the text clearly displays a central feature of most Semitic poetry—parallelism. That is, the ancient poet often expresses a closely related or indeed the same idea in adjacent lines—or even within a single line. For example:

> Your goats will bear triplets, your ewes twins,
> Your laden donkey will outrun any mule,
> Your team of horses will gallop in glory,
> No ox will be a match for yours at the yoke.
>
> (Tablet VI 19–22)

or

> Enkidu, eat the bread; it is the staff of life.
> Drink the ale; it is the custom of the land.
>
> (Tablet II 27–28)

or

> My friend, who was like a wild ass on the run,
> An upland donkey, a leopard in the wild,
> My friend Enkidu, a wild ass on the run,
> An upland donkey, a leopard in the wild—
> My friend Enkidu, he and I teamed up.
>
> (Tablet X 124–28)

Blanket repetition is also frequent in Akkadian epic, with entire passages reused in similar circumstances. Note, for example, the lines describing the travelers' settling in for the night and the dreams of Gilgamesh in Tablet IV (e.g., ll. 10ff.) and the hero's recapitulation of his and Enkidu's back story to those whom he encounters in Tablets X and XI (e.g., Tablet X 47ff.).

As a rule, Akkadian epic style favors description over action. Consider the elaborate picture the poet draws here of the Cedar Forest. Even when he employs active verbs, he adduces recurrent and continuing activities that one might expect to observe upon any visit to the awesome site:

> They gazed at Cedar Mountain, throne of the gods,
> Seat of goddesses, its great expanse

Shrouded with cool and fragrant shade,
The trees tangled with thickets of thorn
Under an arching canopy. Cedar saplings
Grew around the perimeter one league deep,
And cypresses for another two-thirds of a league.
The cedar bark was scabby with resin
Up to sixty cubits high, and the oozing sap
Dribbled down like raindrops into ravines.
Birds began to sing throughout the forest,
Answering each other, a constant din.
Cicadas joined in, chirping in chorus.
A wood pigeon moaned, a turtle dove called back.
The cries of storks and of francolins
Made the forest exult, the woodland rejoice.
Monkey mothers were crooning, and their young
Shrieked in unison. It was like a band of musicians
Beating out rhythms every day for Humbaba.

(Tablet V 6–24)

To this compare the concise manner in which the poet concludes the battle
with Humbaba:

Gilgamesh heard his friend. He pulled out
The long dagger that hung from his belt
And struck Humbaba deep in the neck.
Enkidu helped him to pull out his lungs,
And then Gilgamesh leapt up
And cut the tusks from his jaws as a trophy.

(Tablet V 157–62)

Enkidu and Gilgamesh

Enkidu's relationship to Gilgamesh can usefully be described as one which
literary critics refer to as a doppelgänger, or "double." That is, in some ways
the two figures can be seen as representing complementary sides of a single
personality. For instance, we see that the life path of Enkidu that carries him
from wild man to civilized individual is followed in reverse by Gilgamesh,

when in extreme mourning for his lost comrade he abandons his fine garments for animal skins and departs Uruk for aimless wandering in the wilderness. In turn, this process is undone in preparation for Gilgamesh's return to his city and kingship, when he recapitulates the civilizing of Enkidu by bathing and donning his royal finery:

> Then Urshanabi led Gilgamesh to the washtub,
> And Gilgamesh washed his matted hair clean.
> He threw his old pelts into the sea
> And soaked in the tub until his skin glowed.
> He had a new headband made for him to wear,
> And royal robes that suited his dignity.
>
> (Tablet XI 257–62)

Note also that on the way to the Cedar Forest the two characters alternate in providing encouragement to one another. When one becomes fainthearted and bewails the dangers ahead, the other cites previous successful undertakings in promising a favorable outcome of the expedition. This can be seen as the churning and recursive consideration of contradictory aspects of a problem within a single anxious mind.

As many writers have lately observed, homoeroticism is an aspect of the relationship between the two adventurers, as demonstrated by the repeated prediction that Gilgamesh would be "drawn to it [the meteor symbolic of Enkidu] as by the love of a woman" (e.g., Tablet I 199) and by his veiling his dead friend's face "as if it were his bride's" (Tablet VIII 56). But this begs the question of how much we should make of this, for a gay identity would be an anachronism in ancient Mesopotamia. After all, the basic heterosexuality of the king and his sexual abuse of his female subjects are a major motivating factor early in the narrative (Tablet I 65–66). Rather, the intense love of Gilgamesh for his comrade underlines the intimate bond between the friends. The excruciating grief from which Gilgamesh suffers following the demise of Enkidu is caused not only by the realization that he will ultimately share the latter's fate, but also by the loss of his dearest one.

Dreams

A major structural element of the Standard Babylonian Gilgamesh Epic is the reporting of dreams. Through their anticipation of future events, which unfailingly come to pass as foreseen, these dreams propel the narrative forward. These nocturnal visions always require interpretation by someone other than the dreamer himself. The interpreter need not be someone with special training in such explication: "Though born in the wild, Enkidu knew / How to give counsel. He interpreted the dream" (Tablet IV 26–27).

Ring Structure

Within its historical and literary context the Standard Babylonian Gilgamesh Epic is a quite sophisticated and thereby very unusual work. Perhaps the most striking feature is what critics refer to as a "ring narrative," which encompasses the text. At the beginning of Tablet I, the poet invites the listener/reader to ascend and inspect the fortifications of Uruk and to view the city itself.

> Climb the walls of Uruk and walk along them.
> Examine the massive, terraced foundations.
> Is the masonry not of fine, fired bricks?
> Those foundations were laid by the Seven Sages.
> One square mile is town, one square mile orchard,
> One square mile clay-pits, and half a square mile
> Is devoted to Eanna, its buildings and temples.
> These four parts make up the city of Uruk.
>
> (Tablet I 16–23)

The closing lines of the poem are almost identical to these verses, modified only slightly to fit their new context as an address by Gilgamesh to the ferryman Urshanabi, who has accompanied the king on his homecoming to Uruk:

> O Urshanabi, climb Uruk's walls and walk along them.
> Examine the massive, terraced foundations.
> Is the masonry not of fine, fired bricks?
> Those foundations were laid by the Seven Sages.
> One square mile is town, one square mile orchard,

One square mile clay-pits, and half a square mile
The temple of Ishtar. Three square miles and a half
    Is the area of Uruk.

    (Tablet XI 318–25)

Furthermore, the Epic constitutes a veritable sampler of Mesopotamian literary genres. Included are entire or excerpted examples of elegy (Tablet X 271–95), lament (Tablet VIII 1–53), mythic narrative (Tablet XI 10–198), proverb (Tablet V 51–53), folktale (Tablet VI 48–69, Tablet XI 300–302), curse (Tablet V 152–53, Tablet VII 74–102), and even a parody of a royal inscription (Tablet VII 44–46). This sophistication contributes greatly to the appeal that the Epic has for modern readers and undoubtedly had for Babylonians as well.

Females in the Gilgamesh Epic

Here I leave aside minor figures such as the members of the divine court in the netherworld, who exercise little or no influence on the development of the plot (see the Glossary of Deities, Persons, and Places). With the exception of Ishtar, who as so often in Akkadian literature represents the dangers of unbridled sexuality, in the Epic major female characters, women and goddesses alike, perform roles befitting the position of women in a patriarchal society. These females do not display much in the way of agency. Gilgamesh's mother Ninsun dispenses wise advice in explicating his dreams (Tablet I 203ff.) and exploits her position as a deity to request special attention for her son from higher authority (Tablet III 34ff.). Aya, wife of Shamash, is implored to nag her husband to make sure he abides by Ninsun's desires (Tablet III 52–54, 65ff.). Shiduri the tavern-keeper provides the hero with a shoulder to cry on (Tablet X). The wife of Utanapishtim, who is not even dignified with a personal name, merely serves to hear her husband's remarks (Tablet XI 204–6) and to bake the cakes that prove to Gilgamesh that he had indeed been asleep for a week (Tablet XI 212ff.).

Only the harlot Shamhat, albeit at the instruction of the king and explicitly exercising "all that a woman knows" (Tablet I 141, 146), performs a crucial function within the narrative by taming the primeval wild man Enkidu and introducing him to human mores.

The Moral of the Story?

Like any great work of literature, the Standard Babylonian Gilgamesh Epic encompasses many meanings. As in most premodern heroic narratives, the hero's primary motivation is the desire for lasting fame. Despite his initial realization that death is inevitable ("Men's days are numbered. Whatever we do/ It is like a puff of wind, gone and no more," Tablet II 134–35), Gilgamesh is "a man without any cares" (Tablet I 181). He proposes to achieve a kind of immortality through memorable deeds ("Let my journey begin. I will fell the cedar / And make for myself an eternal name!" Tablet II 161–62).

However, the death of his partner drives home to Gilgamesh the unbearable fact that he too will someday perish:

> Then I became afraid that I would die too,
> Terrified of death, and so I wander the wild.
> What happened to my friend was too much for me,
> And so I wander far, wander far in the wild.
>
> (Tablet X 57–60)

> Will I not die some day and be just like Enkidu?
> My heart is pierced through with sorrow!
> I am afraid of death, and so I wander the wild
> Searching for Utanapishtim, son of Ubar-Tutu.
>
> (Tablet IX 3–6)

On his way to Utanapishtim, Gilgamesh is admonished as to the futility of his quest by his patron, the Sun God: "Where are you wandering, Gilgamesh? / You will never find the life you are seeking" (Tablet IX 22–23). Nonetheless the hero bluffs and bullies his way past the Scorpion People, the tavern-keeper, and the ferryman to reach his immediate goal, his ancestor Utanapishtim, who duly informs him about the unique circumstances under which he had been granted immortality, adding: "As for you, who will call the gods to assembly / So you can come to have the life you are seeking?" (Tablet XI 199–200).

Having then failed the challenge of conquering sleep—the "little brother of Death," according to the Greeks—Gilgamesh falls into despair:

> "O Utanapishtim, what should I do, where should I go?
> A thief has stolen my body.

Death has moved into my bedroom,
And wherever I go, Death will be with me."

(Tablet XI 238–41)

When he is robbed by a serpent of even the "Heartbeat Plant" that would have conferred upon him (temporary) rejuvenation, the hero laments to his new companion:

"For whom did I work so hard, Urshanabi,
For whom did I drain my heart dry of blood?
I didn't do anything good for myself,
Only did the earth-lion, the snake, a favor."

(Tablet XI 306–9)

The Epic concludes with the lines already quoted above, wherein Gilgamesh utilizes the description of Uruk and its walls—his achievements after all— implicitly to express his pride in his "eternal name" (cf. Tablet II 162).

Since the introduction to the Epic in Tablet I praises the virtues of Gilgamesh as they may be seen after his return from his quest before it launches into a catalogue of his earlier abuses, the ancient reader—or listener—might well see the Epic as a sort of "mirror for princes"—a text in which a malfeasant ruler learns from experience to temper his appetites and to rule in the interests of his subjects as well as his own. But this lesson is less trenchant for a modern woman or man—at least for those not residing in an autocracy. An audience from any period or society, however, will appreciate the hero's struggle to come to terms with his inherent limitations, his ultimate acceptance of his transitory existence as a human being, and his final—at least within this tale—consolation in taking pride in his earthly achievements.

Gary Beckman
University of Michigan

ABOUT THIS EDITION

My goal in approaching the Gilgamesh epic, which I come to as an enthusiast rather than a professional Assyriologist, has been to produce a version that is coherent as English narrative poetry while staying as close as is feasible to the outlines of the original text. The main challenge has been the fragmentary nature of the text as we have it. I have relied throughout upon Andrew George's construction of the Standard Version of the Gilgamesh epic in his Oxford critical edition (2003) as well as the material in his publication (with F.N.H. Al-Rawi, 2014) of the more recently discovered Monkey Tablet, which provides twenty or so additional lines in Tablet V. George's own translation of the Akkadian and Old Babylonian texts (and a bit of prose Hittite at the beginning of Tablet VII) that he has assembled indicates by way of brackets, italics, ellipses, and blank spaces exactly where the fragmentary lines break down and where the lacunas—gaps in the cuneiform tablet manuscripts—large and small, occur. His text, translation, and introductory essays are an invaluable service, indispensable really, to anyone interested in the current state of the Standard Version, the history of its discovery and reconstruction, and its interpretation.

A comparison of my version with the translation in George's edition will show that I have omitted some passages that are too fragmentary to yield continuous meaning, but also that I have adopted many of his conjectures for individual words and phrases that complete the meaning of a given fragmentary line. I have also knitted together other, more substantial, fragmentary passages into coherent scenes, condensed some passages, and have occasionally improvised a transitional line or two that ties together scenes separated by a substantial lacuna. All of this is in the interest of the reader who is better served by a text that reads straight through on a clean page.

In the same spirit, I have eliminated or varied some of the formulaic language and repetition common in the original, keeping, I hope, just enough to represent or at least suggest these stylistic features. Also in the spirit of readability—as well as narrative drive and dramatic shaping—I have arranged the text into verse paragraphs rather than reproducing the couplet, and sometimes triplet and quatrain structures, that are implicit in the Akkadian text. I do retain the couplet structure where it is rhetorically important, as in Gilgamesh's lament for Enkidu in Tablet VIII.

My verse line, typically two main stresses on either side of a central syntactic pause, is intended to be analogous to the original's verse, although I go easy on the alliteration that is an important feature in *Gilgamesh*'s verse line, which in some ways bears an uncanny resemblance to the Old English meter in *Beowulf*. Recitations of passages in the Akkadian compiled by Martin Worthington can be found at http://www.openculture.com/2010/10/the_ sounds_of_ancient_mesopotamia.html. In the main my lines are end-stopped, as in the original, but I do occasionally use strategic enjambment, running a sentence into the next line and then stopping, to keep the movement fluid and for emphatic effect in shaping a scene.

The line numbers in the margin refer my version. The corresponding line numbers in George's edition and in Al-Rawi's and George's edition of Tablet V are given in the Appendix.

Having translated Homer's *Iliad* and *Odyssey* as well as Hesiod's *Theogony* and *Works and Days* earlier in my career, working on *Gilgamesh* has brought home to me as nothing else has the cogency of Martin West's thesis in his monumental *The East Face of Helicon: West Asiatic Elements in Greek Poetry and Myth* (Oxford, 1997), a book that has been justly hailed as one of the most important works in classical studies of our generation. West argues in manifold and convincing detail that early Greek culture in general—and poetry especially— are deeply indebted to Mesopotamian and other Near Eastern precedents, and he traces the lines of cultural transmission from east to west. His chapters on Homeric epic expose many stylistic features—formulas, similes, speech patterns, narrative motifs and structures—that *Iliad* and *Odyssey* have in common with *Gilgamesh*; he also lays out the greater case that the Akkadian epic is structurally and thematically both Iliadic and Odyssean. In the first part of the poem the hero Gilgamesh is a literary ancestor of Achilles, with a divine mother who intercedes for him and a beloved friend whom he loses to a death he mourns elaborately and cannot accept. In the latter half he becomes a primordial Odysseus, a solar hero in his journey through the dark and over the sea and finally back to his original home. Readers who catch echoes of my translations of Greek epic in my rendering of *Gilgamesh* should not be surprised.

I am indebted to Gary Beckman not only for his splendid Introduction; Glossary of Deities, Persons, and Places; and Suggestions for Further Reading, but also for the many suggestions and corrections he made to improve the manuscript. My thanks also to an anonymous reader for an early critical reading of my version of Tablet I that both encouraged me and got me on the right track. And I am grateful to Cara Polsley and Erland Crupper for reading and commenting on the entire manuscript. My special thanks to Paula Console for teaching an early draft to her students at Donnelly College and giving me feedback. Brian Rak, my longtime friend and editor at Hackett, is responsible, among his other ministrations, for motivating me to start learning Akkadian and working on *Gilgamesh*. I'm grateful to him. And to my wife, Judy Roitman, who has, as ever, sustained me in the work.

—Stanley Lombardo

TIMELINE

Beginning Date	Ending Date		
ca. 2600 BCE		Sumerian First Dynasty of Ur	(1) A possible human ruler named Bilgames may have lived around 2600 BCE; an extant royal inscription from about this time mentions a king of Kish named Enmebaragesi, who lived around 2600 BCE (see below). (2) A minor deity named Bilgames, later held to be an ancestor of the rulers of the Third Dynasty of Ur, is also attested in a Sumerian text from this period.
2112 BCE	2004 BCE	Sumerian Third Dynasty of Ur	(1) The Sumerian King List, which dates from this period, purports to list kings of the First Dynasty of Ur. Among them, in sixth place, is Bilgames. (2) Royal hymns from this period claim that the Third Dynasty's King Shulgi is a brother of the deity Bilgames. (3) The Sumerian King List mentions a king of Kish named Enmebaragesi, father of Aka. Aka is otherwise known as an enemy of Bilgames in one of the five extant Sumerian Bilgames tales.
1800 BCE	1600 BCE	Old Babylonian Period	(1) Oral Sumerian Bilgames tales are preserved by Babylonian scribes. (2) A distinctive Akkadian Gilgamesh Epic is recorded. (3) Hammurabi reigns from ca.1792 to ca.1750 BCE.

Beginning Date	Ending Date		
ca. 1200 BCE		The Standard Babylonian Gilgamesh Epic Takes Shape	What has survived as the best-known version of the Gilgamesh epic is attributed to Sîn-lēqi-unninni, a Babylonian sage from an earlier era.
911 BCE	609 BCE	Neo-Assyrian Empire	In this period, Akkadian cuneiform is retained for many governmental and prestige purposes (such as wall reliefs) but business is increasingly documented in Aramaic-language documents written in Aramaic script on perishable materials, of which few examples survive.
800 BCE	700 BCE	Earliest Preserved Tablets Attesting the Standard Babylonian Gilgamesh Epic	The Gilgamesh tablets dating from this period record texts composed several hundred years earlier.
722 BCE	705 BCE	Reign of Sargon II	Dur-Sharrukin, a royal city built expressly for the Assyrian king Sargon II, is abandoned immediately after his death in battle. His successor Sennacherib makes Nineveh, ca.12 miles south, the new royal city.

Beginning Date	Ending Date		
668 BCE	627 BCE	Reign of Ashurbanipal	The library of Ashurbanipal, one of the last Assyrian kings, in Nineveh (outside present-day Mosul) collects thousands of clay tablets preserving the Babylonian literary heritage.
626 BCE	539 BCE	Neo-Babylonian Empire	This period sees a renaissance of the Old Babylonian cultural traditions, especially under the reign of King Nebuchadnezzar II (ca. 605 to ca. 561 BCE), though Aramaic remains the spoken language.
539 BCE		Neo-Babylonian Empire Falls to the Persian Empire	Cyrus the Great of the Achaemenid (Persian) Empire conquers Babylonia. The Persians employ Aramaic as their administrative language.
330 BCE		Alexander the Great of Macedonia Defeats the Persian Empire	Alexander's conquests usher in the Hellenistic era, which spreads Greek culture throughout Mesopotamia.
27 BCE		Caesar Augustus Inaugurates the Roman Empire	With his defeat of Antony and Cleopatra in the Battle of Actium, Caesar Augustus (Octavian) annexes Egypt, and the Roman Republic becomes the Roman Empire.
ca. 100		Extinction of Cuneiform Literacy	Greek and Roman literary traditions having eclipsed those of Mesopotamia, cuneiform literacy is lost for more than 1700 years.

Beginning Date	Ending Date		
1842	1844	Botta Excavates Khorsabad	Paul-Émile Botta, a French diplomat, excavates Khorsabad and uncovers remains of Dur-Sharrukin, royal city of Assyrian ruler Sargon II (722–705 BCE).
1845	1847	Layard Excavates Kuyunjik	Austen Henry Layard, a British diplomat, excavates the mound of Kuyunjik near Mosul, where he uncovers the remains of Nineveh, including the library of the Assyrian king Ashurbanipal. Clay tablets and fragments from the library are shipped to the British Museum in London.
1857		Decipherment of Cuneiform	Independent efforts by amateur and professional scholars from England, Ireland, France, and Germany studying clay tablet fragments held by the British Museum collectively succeed in breaking the code of the cuneiform writing system.
1872		Smith Presents *The Chaldean Account of Genesis*	Amateur cuneiform scholar George Smith recognizes parallels in the Biblical account of Noah's flood and that of a similar flood described in Tablet XI of the Babylonian version of the Gilgamesh epic and presents his sensational findings to the Society of Biblical Archaeology in London. In 1876 he publishes his translation of Tablet XI to great acclaim under the title *The Chaldean Account of Genesis*.
1884	1930	Publication of Editions of the Text of the Babylonian Gilgamesh Epic	German scholar and professor of Semitic languages at Johns Hopkins University Paul Haupt begins publishing his edition of the known text of twelve tablets of the Standard Babylonian Gilgamesh Epic as *Das babylonische Nimrodepos*. In 1930, British archaeologist R.C. Campbell Thompson publishes expanded version of the twelve tablets of the epic.

Beginning Date	Ending Date		
2003		U.S. Invasion of Iraq	The U.S.-led invasion of Iraq results in widespread looting of antiquities, most notably from the Iraq Museum in Baghdad, where more than thirteen thousand objects are stolen.
2003		George Publishes New Edition of Gilgamesh	Professor Andrew George of the School of Oriental and African Studies (SOAS) of the University of London publishes the most complete edition of the epic to date, accounting for an estimated eighty percent of the text of the Standard Babylonian version.
2011		Al-Rawi Discovers the "Monkey Tablet"	Under direction of the Sulaymaniyah Museum in Kurdistani Iraq, Professor Farouk Al-Rawi of SOAS University of London buys back antiquities looted after the U.S. invasion of Iraq, discovering a tablet with previously unknown lines from Tablet V of the Standard Babylonian Gilgamesh Epic that provide a fuller description of the fauna of the Cedar Forest.
2014		Al-Rawi and George Publish Content of the "Monkey Tablet"	In their *Journal of Cuneiform Studies* article "Back to the Cedar Forest: The Beginning and End of Tablet V of the Standard Babylonian Epic of Gilgamesh," Farouk Al-Rawi and Andrew George include the text, a translation, and a discussion of the newly discovered "Monkey Tablet."

The Epic of
GILGAMESH

TABLET I

The Creation of Enkidu

GILGAMESH, who saw the Abyss—
This was the man who understood all, who traveled
To every country on earth, who came to know the depths
Of the world's mysteries, all its dark, secret places,
And brought us a tale of the time before the Flood.
He journeyed far, returned home weary,
And carved all his trials on a tablet of stone.

It was he who built the great walls of Uruk,
Built the wall of Eanna, Ishtar's pure storehouse.
You can still see it all, the outer wall's cornice   *10*
Gleaming like copper in the sun, the inner wall
Beyond all comparison. Run your hands
Over the threshold, feel how ancient it is.
Approach Eanna, the temple of Ishtar.
No king today could ever build their equal.
Climb the walls of Uruk and walk along them.
Examine the massive, terraced foundations.
Is the masonry not of fine, fired bricks?
Those foundations were laid by the Seven Sages.
One square mile is town, one square mile orchard,   *20*
One square mile clay-pits, and half a square mile

Is devoted to Eanna, its buildings and temples.
These four parts make up the city of Uruk.

Go there, approach the cedar ark, unfasten
The lid's bronze latches, and take out the tablet
Of lapis lazuli so you can read aloud
All the ordeals that Gilgamesh endured.

Gilgamesh was greater than all other kings,
Hero of Uruk, a raging bull of a man,
Vanguard of the army when he went to the front,   30
A man all could trust when he brought up the rear.
On defense he was like a great river bank;
On attack, a flood-surge smashing stone walls,
The wild bull of Lugalbanda, paragon of strength,
Nursling of divine Ninsun, the revered Wild Cow.
Gilgamesh was tall, magnificent, terrifying.
He opened passes in the high mountains,
Dug wells on their slopes, crossed the wide sea,
The ocean lit by the rising sun. He roamed the world
In his quest for life, and forced his way through   40
To Utanapishtim the Distant, who survived the Flood.
Gilgamesh rebuilt the altars the Flood destroyed,
And established the rites for men under heaven.

Who can rival Gilgamesh? Who can stand
Against him and say, "I am the king?"
He was called Gilgamesh the day he was born,
One part human and two parts divine.
The Divine Mother drew his figure,
And the god Ea fashioned his body.
His feet were three cubits long, his leg   50
Half a rod in length, six cubits to his stride.
His cheeks were bearded, and the hair
On his head grew as thick as barley,
A man of perfect beauty, earth's most handsome man.

Now he strides like a wild bull, head held high,
Through Uruk the Sheepfold. Gilgamesh
Has no equal when he brandishes his weapons.
He harries all of the young men in Uruk;
No son is left at home with his father;
Day and night his arrogance is unbounded.   60
The people complained, were heard to mutter:

"This is the city's shepherd, this our wise, noble king?
He leaves no daughter at home with her mother.
This is a king, the shepherd of his people?
Gilgamesh leaves no bride to her bridegroom,
No warrior's daughter, no wife to a noble.
This is the city's shepherd, our noble, wise king?"

Anu heard their complaints, their lamentation,
The gods in heaven heard and cried to Aruru,
The Creator Goddess.
                    "You made him, Aruru!   70
Now create his equal, his reflection, his double,
A stormy heart to match his own stormy heart.
Let them fight it out and leave Uruk in peace."

Aruru heard this, and she formed
Within her heart what Anu had in mind.
Then she rinsed her hands in water,
Pinched off a piece of clay and let it fall
Into the wild, and great Enkidu was born.
His power was like the power of the War God,
Of Ninurta himself. His skin was rough, his hair   80
As long as a woman's, waving like Nisaba's,
The Goddess of Grain. Hair matted his body,
Like Sumuqan's, the God of Cattle. He knew nothing
Of human ways, nothing of cultivated fields.
He ate grass in the hills, grazing with gazelles,

And crouched with animals at the watering hole,
Drinking his fill along with herds of wild game.

One day a hunter met him at a watering hole
Where the wild herds were drinking, for they had roamed
Into his territory. Three days in a row   *90*
He met him there, staring into his eyes, numb with fear.
When at last he returned home with his catch
He was dazed, terrified, his face haggard with fatigue,
And he opened his mouth and said to his father:

"Father, there is a strange man, unlike any other,
Who comes down from the hills, the strongest man alive,
As strong as a rock come down from the sky.
He ranges the hills with wild animals, eating grass
And coming through the land to drink from the pools.
I am afraid to go near him. He fills in the pits   *100*
That I dig and tears up the traps I set, letting
The game escape and slip through my grasp.
He stops me from doing my work in the wild."

The hunter's father then said to his son:

"Gilgamesh of Uruk has never known defeat.
He is as strong as a rock from the sky. Go to Uruk
And praise this wild man's strength before Gilgamesh.
Ask him to give you a prostitute
To come back with you here, so that a woman
Can overpower this man. When he comes down next   *110*
To the drinking hole, have her strip naked there.
When he sees her enticing him he will lie with her,
And the beasts of the wild will then reject him."

So the hunter set out and journeyed to Uruk.
He presented himself to Gilgamesh, saying:

"There is a strange man, unlike any other,
Roaming the countryside. He is as strong as a rock
Come down from heaven. He roams the hills
All day with the herds and leaves his tracks
By the water hole. I am afraid to go near him.   *120*
He fills in the pits I dig and tears up my traps
And stops me from doing my work in the wild."

And Gilgamesh said:
                    "Hunter, go back,
And take with you Shamhat. Have her strip
At the drinking hole, and when he sees her
Beckoning him he will lie down with her,
And the beasts of the wild will then reject him."

So the hunter took Shamhat back with him.
In three days they came to the drinking hole
And sat down there side by side, waiting   *130*
For the wild game to come. Two days passed,
And on the third day the herds of gazelles
Came down to drink, and Enkidu was with them.
The animals were glad for the water, as was Enkidu,
Who was born in the hills and grazed with gazelles.
And the woman saw him, saw the wild man
Who had come from the hills. The hunter said to her:

"There he is, Shamhat. Now bare your breasts, have no fear,
Entice him, let him see you naked and possess your body.
When he comes close take off your clothes and lie with him.   *140*
Do for this man all that a woman knows.
Once he mingles in love with you, the wild beasts
That roamed the hills with him will reject him."

She was not afraid to take him. She stripped bare
And embraced his wildness, and as he lay on her
She did for him all that a woman knows.

Six days and seven nights they lay together,
Enkidu oblivious of his home in the hills.
When he had enough he went back to his herd,
But when the gazelles saw him they bolted off,   *150*
When the wild creatures saw him they sprinted away.
Enkidu tried to follow, but his body was in knots,
And his knees buckled when he started to run,
All his speed lost, and all the animals gone.
Enkidu had grown weak; he had begun to think,
And the thoughts of a man were now in his heart.
He went back to the woman, sat at her feet, watched her,
And listened carefully to what she had to say:

"You are handsome, Enkidu, just like a god.
Why do you want to run with beasts in the hills?   *160*
Come with me, and I will take you to Uruk
With its strong walls, take you to the city
And the sacred temple of Anu and Ishtar.
Gilgamesh lives there. He is immensely strong
And lords it over the city like a raging bull."

Enkidu liked what he heard. He longed for a friend,
Someone who could understand his heart. He said:

"Take me to that holy temple, woman,
To the house of Anu and Ishtar. Take me
To the city where Gilgamesh is lord.   *170*
I will challenge him openly, cry aloud in Uruk,
'I am the strongest here, come to change everything.
I was born in the hills and am the strongest of all!'"

She said:
            "Then let's go, so he can see your face.
I know very well where Gilgamesh lives in Uruk.
Enkidu, the young men there wear beautiful belts;
Every day is a festival, drums beating a rhythm.
The girls are lovely, and they all smell so sweet.

Even the elders get out of their beds for them!
O Enkidu, you who love life, I will show you   *180*
Gilgamesh, a man without any cares.
You will see him yourself in his glowing manhood,
His perfect body, so masculine and strong.
He is stronger than you, and does not need sleep.
Shamash, the glorious Sun God, has favored him;
And Anu, the Sky God, and Enlil,
And wise Ea have given him deep understanding.
I tell you, even before you leave these wild lands,
Gilgamesh will know in his dreams you are coming."

And Gilgamesh had a dream. He woke up to tell   *190*
His mother, Ninsun, an all-wise goddess, and said:

"Mother, I had a dream last night. In my dream
I walked at night under the stars of heaven.
One of the stars fell down from the sky,
Like a rock from heaven. I tried to lift it,
But it was too heavy. All the people in Uruk
Came out to see it, crowds of commoners jostling
And nobles who came up to kiss the star's feet.
I was drawn to it as by the love of a woman,
I caressed it, embraced it, and finally lifted it   *200*
And brought it to you, set it before your feet,
And you said that this star was my match, my equal."

And Ninsun, shrewd and wise, said to her son:

"This star that fell like a rock from heaven
And that you tried to lift but found too heavy
And that would not budge when you tried to move it,
But finally you lifted it and set it down at my feet,
And I told you that this star was your match, your equal,
And you were drawn to it as to a woman,
You caressed it, loved and embraced it—this star   *210*
Is a strong comrade who will come to help you.

He is the strongest of all the wild creatures,
As mighty as a rock from heaven. You will be glad
When you see him, you will love him as a woman,
And he will be your true friend and often save you."

Gilgamesh had another dream. He rose
And went in to his divine mother, and said:

"Mother, I have had another dream.
An axe lay in the main street of Uruk.
A strange thing, and a crowd gathered around.   *220*
The whole city of Uruk came out to see it.
When I saw it I was glad. I bent down, drawn to it.
I loved it like a woman and wore it at my side."

And Gilgamesh's mother, the goddess Ninsun,
Wise in all things, said to her son:

"My son, the axe that you saw in your dream
And that drew you to it like the love of a woman,
That is the comrade I will give you. He will come
As mighty as a star that falls from the sky,
A brave companion who will help his friend in need."   *230*

And Gilgamesh then said to his mother:

"May this friend come from Enlil to help me,
And I will help him, and will be his friend."

So Gilgamesh told his dreams to his mother
While Shamhat and Enkidu were making love.

TABLET II

Gilgamesh Befriends Enkidu

While the two of them were making love,
Enkidu forgot his home in the wilderness.
For seven days and seven nights Enkidu
Was erect, inside Shamhat the harlot.

Then she opened her mouth and said to him:

"You look like a god to me, Enkidu.
Why should you run wild with the beasts again?
Come, I will lead you to Uruk's town square,
To the sacred precinct, home of Anu.
Get up, Enkidu, and let me take you there,   *10*
To Eanna, the temple where Anu dwells
And men are busy about their trades."

Enkidu listened, and her advice, the words
Of this woman, seemed good to him.
Shamhat then divided her clothing, giving half
To Enkidu and wearing the other half herself.
She led him like a god to the sheepherders' tents.
The shepherds all crowded around
And talked about him among themselves:

"This fellow is built just like Gilgamesh,   *20*
As solid and big as a fort! It must be Enkidu,
Born in the hills, strong as a rock from the sky."

They served him bread and ale, but Enkidu only knew
How to suck milk from wild animals. He gaped
And fumbled about, unsure how to eat the bread
Or drink the strong ale. Then the woman said:

"Enkidu, eat the bread; it is the staff of life.
Drink the ale; it is the custom of the land."

So Enkidu ate until he was full, and he drank
Seven cups of strong ale. He became cheery,   *30*
His heart soared, and his face was radiant.
He rubbed down his matted hair and skin with oil.
Enkidu had turned into a man, and when he dressed
In a man's clothing he looked like a young warrior.
He began to carry weapons for hunting lions
So the herdsmen could get some rest at night,
And he caught wolves too. The shepherds slept well,
For Enkidu, unmatched in strength, was their watchman.

One day while Enkidu was making love to Shamhat
He happened to look up and saw someone coming.   *40*
He said to the woman:
                    "Shamhat, bring that man here.
I want to know where he is going."

She went to the man and asked him where he was going,
And he answered, addressing Enkidu:

"Someone I know is getting married,
And I am going to the wedding banquet.
I will spread out a feast on the ritual table,
Delicious food for all the wedding guests.
Then for Gilgamesh, for the king of Uruk,

The curtain will be opened, the veil parted. *50*
Gilgamesh will use his right of first choice.
He will couple first with the bride,
And the bridegroom will come after.
This is Gilgamesh's birthright, ordained by the gods
When his umbilical cord was cut."

When Enkidu heard this, his face grew pale,
And he strode forward angrily, with Shamhat behind.
He entered the great marketplace of Uruk,
And a crowd thronged around him where he stood.
Saying things like:
        "He is the spitting image of Gilgamesh." *60*
"No, he is shorter." "But his bones are thicker."
"He was reared on wild beasts' milk. He is stronger."

And,
      "Gilgamesh has finally met his match.
This is the great one, a hero as beautiful
As a god, a match even for Gilgamesh."

Somewhere in Uruk, a bridal bed was made,
Fit for the Goddess of Love. The bride was waiting
For the bridegroom, but in the dark of night
Gilgamesh got up and came to the house.
Then Enkidu stepped forward, standing in the street *70*
To block his way. Great Gilgamesh came on
And Enkidu met him at the gate. He spread his feet wide
And stopped Gilgamesh from entering the house.
Closing on each other, like bulls locking horns,
They shattered the doorposts, and the walls shook.
As they struggled Gilgamesh went down on one knee,
His foot firmly planted on the ground.
As soon as he had done so his fury subsided,
And Enkidu said to him,

"There is not another like you in all the world.   *80*
Ninsun, who is as strong as a wild ox herself,
Is the mother who bore you, and now you are above
All other men, and Enlil has made you king!"

Then they kissed each other, sealing their friendship.

And Gilgamesh took Enkidu to his mother, saying,

"He is the strongest man in the country,
Like a rock from the sky, massive as a fort."

But his mother, wise Ninsun, responded,

"Enkidu has no father or mother,
His hair is shaggy.   *90*
He was born in the wild and has no one at all."

Enkidu was standing there. He heard what she said
And pondered it. His eyes filled with tears,
And his limbs went slack. The two men held each other,
Their hands clasped, and then Gilgamesh said,

"My friend, why do your eyes fill with tears?
Why is your heart sick? Why are you sighing?"

And Enkidu answered, saying to Gilgamesh,

"My friend, my voice is choked in my throat,
My arms are limp, and my legs are trembling.   *100*
My strength is all gone, and my heart filled with fear."

Gilgamesh thought, and then said to Enkidu:

"I know what we can do, Enkidu. Humbaba,
Have you heard of ferocious Humbaba?

Let's kill him, Enkidu, destroy his power,
Surprise him in his lair in the Cedar Forest!"

Enkidu opened his mouth and answered Gilgamesh:

"I learned about Humbaba, my friend,
When I wandered up in the hills with the herds.
The Cedar Forest is sixty leagues of wilderness.   *110*
Who would dare to enter that forest?
Humbaba's voice is a flood, his speech is fire,
He breathes out death. Why do you want to do this?
This is a fight that cannot be won."

Gilgamesh answered,
                    "I will climb
The slopes of that forest, my friend."

But Enkidu went on,
                    "How can we go there?
Enlil made Humbaba a terror to men
To keep the cedars safe in the forest.
That is not a journey that men should make,   *120*
That is not someone that men should look at.
Adad the Storm God is first, Humbaba second.
His shout is a flood, his speech is fire,
He breathes out death. For sixty leagues
He hears every whisper of sound in the forest.
Who among the great gods of heaven,
Would oppose Humbaba? Enlil made him
As a terror to men to protect the cedars.
If you enter his forest you will tremble with fear."

And Gilgamesh answered Enkidu: *130*

"Why are you whimpering like this, my friend?
My heart grieves at your cowardly words.

Only the gods live forever in daylight.
Men's days are numbered. Whatever we do
It is like a puff of wind, gone and no more.
Why are you afraid of death now?
You were born and bred in the wilderness.
Even the lions feared you. Grown men
Ran away from you. You have seen it all,
Your heart is tried and true, tested in combat.   *140*
Come, my friend, we're off to the forge
To watch them cast axes and hatchets for us!"

Hand in hand they headed to the forge.
The smiths sat down, talking things over.
Then they cast huge hatchets, and axes that weighed
Three talents each. They cast great swords
With two talents of metal in each blade,
A half-talent in the knobs on the hilts,
And sheaths that contained a half-talent of gold.
Each hero carried a half-ton of weapons.   *150*

Then Gilgamesh bolted Uruk's seven gates
And called an assembly. The people gathered,
And Gilgamesh, seated on his throne,
Spoke before them, addressing the elders:

"Hear me, elders of Uruk!
I am setting out to face ferocious Humbaba,
To see the god of whom all men talk,
Whose name is repeated in all the lands.
I will destroy him in the Cedar Forest
So all will know Uruk's offshoot is great.   *160*
Let my journey begin. I will fell the cedar
And make for myself an eternal name!"

Then Gilgamesh turned to the young men of Uruk:

"Hear me now, young men of Uruk,
Men who understand war!
I am heading out boldly to attack Humbaba,
A battle I don't know I will win.
I will travel a road unknown to me.
Give me your blessing as I set out,
And may I see you again when I return   *170*
In triumph through the gate of Uruk.
When I return I will celebrate
The New Year festival twice that year.
Let the festivities begin!
Let the drums boom before the goddess Ninsun!"

Then Enkidu warned the council of elders
And the young men too, warriors of Uruk:

"Tell him not to go to the Cedar Forest.
That is not a journey that men should make,
That is not someone that men should look at.   *180*
The guardian of that forest has a long reach.
This Humbaba, his shout is a flood,
His speech is fire, he breathes out death.
For sixty leagues he hears every sound in his forest.
Enlil made Humbaba a terror to men
To keep the cedars safe in the forest.
Adad the Storm God is first, Humbaba second.
Whoever enters his forest will tremble with fear."

The council of elders rose up
And offered this advice to Gilgamesh: *190*

"You are young, Gilgamesh, ruled by emotion,
And you do not understand what you are saying.
This Humbaba, his shout is a deluge,
His speech is fire, he breathes out death.
For sixty leagues he hears every sound in his forest.

Who would dare to enter that forest?
Which of the great gods would quarrel with him?
Adad the Storm God is first, Humbaba second.
Enlil made Humbaba a terror to men
To keep the cedars safe in the forest."   *200*

When he heard this from the council of elders
Gilgamesh laughed and looked at Enkidu.

TABLET III

Preparations for the Journey

Then the elders of Uruk spoke to Gilgamesh:
"Come back to Uruk's dock safe and sound,
And do not trust to your strength alone.
Be wary, Gilgamesh, and make every blow count.
A good man out front saves his companion,
One who knows the way is a shield for his friend.
Let Enkidu go out in front before you.
He knows the way to the Cedar Forest,
And he is a warrior, hardened in combat.
Enkidu will bring you safely back home."   *10*

Then they turned to Enkidu and said,

"Our council entrusts the King to your care.
Bring him back, Enkidu, and return our trust."

Gilgamesh then turned to Enkidu and said,

"Let us go, brother, to the high temple, Egalmah,
And stand before the great Queen Ninsun,
Ninsun who is wise in all manner of things.
She will set our feet on a prudent path."

Gilgamesh and Enkidu clasped hands
And walked together up to the high temple   *20*
And stood before the great Queen Ninsun.
Gilgamesh drew nearer and said to her:

"My heart is set, Ninsun, on making
The long journey to the home of Humbaba.
I will face a battle that I cannot know
And walk a path that is unknown to me.
I ask for your blessing upon my journey.
Allow me to see your face again
And come back in joy through Uruk's gate.
When I return I will celebrate   *30*
The New Year festival twice over again.
We will let the festivities continue,
The drums boom for the goddess Ninsun!"

Ninsun listened with great sadness
To her son Gilgamesh. Then she bathed
Seven times in tamarisk-scented water,
Put on a fine-spun dress, adorned her breast
With a jewel, and crowned her head with a diadem.
Then she climbed the temple's stairs to the roof,
And there she lit incense in a censer   *40*
In supplication to Shamash the Sun.
Lifting her arms she prayed to the Sun God:

"Why do you curse my son with a restless heart?
Now he will trek to Humbaba's far land,
Face a battle that he cannot know,
Walk a path that is unknown to him.
Every day of his journey there and back,
Until he reaches the Cedar Forest,
Until he kills ferocious Humbaba,
Rids the land of the Evil you loathe,   *50*
Each and every day when you circle the earth,
May your bride Aya, the Goddess of Dawn,

Remind you to safeguard him until nightfall,
Keep him unharmed until evening enfolds him.

"O Shamash, it is you who send forth the herds,
Your brightness gives shape to the world,
Your ruddy glow awakens the beasts in the wild.
The people gather at the coming of your light,
The gods of old, the Annunaki, await you.
May Aya your bride not fear to remind you,   60
'Safeguard him until the night comes.'

"And while my son travels to the Cedar Forest,
Let the days be long, and the nights short,
And let him make camp when evening comes.
And may your bride Aya say to you boldly,

'When Gilgamesh and Enkidu face Humbaba,
O Shamash, rouse the storm winds against him,
Winds from the South, the North, the East, and the West,
Colliding typhoons, cyclones, squalls, hurricanes, tempests.
Tornadoes and gales, twisters and whirlwinds,   70
Thirteen winds to darken Humbaba's face!
And then let Gilgamesh hit home with his weapons.'

"Whenever your fires, Shamash, are kindled,
Turn your face toward me, your supplicant,
Your swift-footed mules shall bear you onward,
A couch will await you for you to take your rest,
Your brother gods will bring food to refresh you
And Aya will dry your face with the hem of her robe."

Then Ninsun renewed her prayer to Shamash:

"Will not Gilgamesh become one of the gods?   80
Will he not share the heavens with you?
Not share a scepter and crown with the moon?
Not grow wise with Ea of the Nether Ocean?

Not rule with Irnina the black-headed people?
Not dwell with Ningishzida in the World Below?"

So Wild Cow Ninsun entreated Shamash,
Ninsun who was wise in all manner of things.
Then she snuffed out the incense, came down from the roof,
Summoned Enkidu, and said this to him:

"Great Enkidu, you did not come from my womb,   *90*
But from now on you will be in the care
Of Gilgamesh's temple women, his priestesses.
And just as these women take in foundlings
And adopt them as their foster children,
So too do I, Enkidu, now take you as my son,
Brother of Gilgamesh, who grants you his favor.
When you travel together to the Cedar Forest,
May the days be long, and the nights short,
And may you triumph by Shamash's will
At the Gate of Marduk in the Cedar Forest!"   *100*

Then Gilgamesh addressed Uruk's officials:

"During our journey to the Cedar Forest
And until we return, do not allow
The young men to assemble in the streets.
Judge yourselves the lawsuits of the weak."

The officials stood, expressed their good wishes,
And the young men of Uruk crowded around,
The officials kissed the feet of Gilgamesh and said:

"Come back to Uruk's dock safe and sound,
And do not trust to your strength alone.   *110*
Be wary, Gilgamesh, and make every blow count.
A good man out front saves his companion,
One who knows the way is a shield for his friend.

Let Enkidu go out in front before you.
He knows the way to the Cedar Forest,
And he is a warrior, hardened in combat.
Enkidu knows the mountain passes,
He will guard his friend and companion,
Enkidu will bring you safely back home."

Then they turned to Enkidu and said,   *120*

"Our council entrusts the King to your care.
Bring him back, Enkidu, and return our trust."

Then Enkidu said to Gilgamesh:

"Let's begin the journey your heart is set on.
Have no fear, and keep your eyes on me.
I know Humbaba, his lair and his ways.
Send this crowd home, and let's move out."

The people were cheered to hear his words,
And the young men shouted:

                              "May your god go with you,
May Shamash help you to win through to the end!"   *130*

And Gilgamesh and Enkidu went forth from Uruk.

TABLET IV

Journey to the Cedar Forest

After sixty miles they stopped to break bread;
Ninety more miles and they pitched camp for the night:
One hundred and fifty miles a day,
In three days a march of a month and a half.

They drew nearer and nearer to Mount Lebanon.

They faced the sun and dug a well
So they could fill their water-skins with fresh water.
Then Gilgamesh climbed a mountain and sifted
An offering of flour as he prayed to the hill-god:

"Send me a dream, Mountain, a good omen, a vision."   *10*

That night Enkidu made a hut for the dream-god,
Setting in a door against the weather.
He made Gilgamesh lie down in a circle he'd drawn,
And lay himself in the doorway, flat as a net.
Gilgamesh drew his knees up to his chin,
And sleep that drifts over all drifted down over him.
At midnight he reached the end of his slumber,
And then he got up and said to his friend:

"Didn't you call me, my friend? What woke me up?
Didn't you touch me? What startled me?   *20*
Did a spirit pass over me? Why am I cold and numb?
It was a dream, my friend. I have had the first dream!
I dreamed we were in a valley, a mountain valley,
It was all confused,
And the mountain fell down on us."

Though born in the wild, Enkidu knew
How to give counsel. He interpreted the dream:

"This is a good dream, my friend, a good omen for us.
The mountain you saw could not be Humbaba.
We will take Humbaba, we will fight and kill him,   *30*
Cast his corpse down on the field of battle.
Tomorrow we will see a good sign from the Sun God."

After sixty miles they stopped to break bread;
Ninety more miles and they pitched camp for the night:
One hundred and fifty miles a day,
In three days a march of a month and a half.

They drew nearer and nearer to Mount Lebanon.

They faced the sun and dug a well
So they could fill their water-skins with fresh water.
Then Gilgamesh climbed a mountain and sifted   *40*
An offering of flour as he prayed to the hill-god:

"Send me a dream, Mountain, a good omen, a vision."

That night Enkidu made a hut for the dream-god,
Setting in a door against the weather.
He made Gilgamesh lie down in a circle he'd drawn,
And lay himself in the doorway, flat as a net.
Gilgamesh drew his knees up to his chin,
And sleep that drifts over all drifted down over him.

At midnight he reached the end of his slumber,
And then he got up and said to his friend: *50*

"Didn't you call me, my friend? What woke me up?
Didn't you touch me? What startled me?
Did a spirit pass over me? Why am I cold and numb?
A dream, I have had a second dream, my friend!
My second dream was better than the first.
In my dream a mountain threw me down,
Threw me down, my friend, and held me by my feet.
Then a bright light appeared and grew more intense,
And out of that light a beautiful man,
The handsomest man in the land, appeared   *60*
And pulled me out from beneath that mountain,
He gave me water to drink and calmed me down,
And then he lifted me onto my feet."

Enkidu spoke to Gilgamesh, saying:

"We will meet Humbaba, and he is not like that,
My friend. He is completely different,
Not like that mountain. You should not be afraid."

After sixty miles they stopped to break bread;
Ninety more miles and they pitched camp for the night:
One hundred and fifty miles a day,   *70*
In three days a march of a month and a half.

They drew nearer and nearer to Mount Lebanon.

They faced the sun and dug a well
So they could fill their water-skins with fresh water.
Then Gilgamesh climbed a mountain and sifted
An offering of flour as he prayed to the hill-god:

"Send me a dream, Mountain, a good omen, a vision."

That night Enkidu made a hut for the dream-god,
Setting in a door against the weather.
He made Gilgamesh lie down in a circle he'd drawn,   *80*
And lay himself in the doorway, flat as a net.
Gilgamesh drew his knees up to his chin,
And sleep that drifts over all drifted down over him.
At midnight he reached the end of his slumber,
And then he got up and said to his friend:

"Didn't you call me, my friend? What woke me up?
Didn't you touch me? What startled me?
Did a spirit pass over me? Why am I cold and numb?
My friend, I have had the third dream!
My dream was confused. An old man was there.   *90*
The heavens roared, the earth rumbled beneath.
The air grew very still, and then it was dark.
Lightning flashed and everything caught fire,
Flames flaring up to the sky, death raining down.
Then the fire went out, and there was ash everywhere.
Let us consider what all this means."

Enkidu told Gilgamesh what his dream meant:

"My friend, your dream is a good omen for us.
We are getting closer and closer to the forest;
Your dreams are closer, and the battle is near.   *100*
Soon you will see the divine, shining auras
Of Humbaba, whom you fear so much.
You will lock horns with him like a bull,
You will batter him, and force his head down.
The old man you saw is the powerful god
Who fathered you, divine Lugalbanda."

After sixty miles they stopped to break bread;
Ninety more miles and they pitched camp for the night:

One hundred and fifty miles a day,
In three days a march of a month and a half.   *110*

They drew nearer and nearer to Mount Lebanon.

They faced the sun and dug a well
So they could fill their water-skins with fresh water.
Then Gilgamesh climbed a mountain and sifted
An offering of flour as he prayed to the hill-god:

"Send me a dream, Mountain, a good omen, a vision."

At night Enkidu made a hut for the dream-god,
Setting in a door against the weather.
He made Gilgamesh lie down in a circle he'd drawn,
And lay himself in the doorway, flat as a net.   *120*
Gilgamesh drew his knees up to his chin,
And sleep that drifts over all drifted down over him.
At midnight he reached the end of his slumber,
And then he got up and said to his friend:

"Didn't you call me, my friend? What woke me up?
Didn't you touch me? What startled me?
Did a spirit pass over me? Why am I cold and numb?
My friend, I have just had a fourth dream!
It is far better than the other three dreams.
I saw a thunderbird flying in the sky,   *130*
Soaring above us, high as a cloud.
Its face was all twisted, its mouth was fire,
And it breathed forth death. There was a man, too,
A strange-looking man standing in my dream.
He bound the bird's wings, and touching my arm,
Threw the bird down right there at my feet."

Then Enkidu explained Gilgamesh's dream:

"You saw a thunderbird flying in the sky,
Soaring above us, high as a cloud.
Its face was all twisted, its mouth was fire,   *140*
And it breathed forth death. You will fear this bird,
Its terrible splendor. But I will catch it,
Catch it by its foot and let you rise up.
The man you saw was mighty Shamash,
This is a good dream, my friend.
Humbaba will be destroyed,
We will bind his arms and stand upon him.
And tomorrow we will see a good sign from the Sun God."

After sixty miles they stopped to break bread;
Ninety more miles and they pitched camp for the night: *150*
One hundred and fifty miles a day,
In three days a march of a month and a half.

They drew nearer and nearer to Mount Lebanon.

They faced the sun and dug a well
So they could fill their water-skins with fresh water.
Then Gilgamesh climbed a mountain and sifted
An offering of flour as he prayed to the hill-god:

"Send me a dream, Mountain, a good omen, a vision."

That night Enkidu made a hut for the dream-god,
Setting in a door against the weather.   *160*
He made Gilgamesh lie down in a circle he'd drawn,
And lay himself in the doorway, flat as a net.
Gilgamesh drew his knees up to his chin,
And sleep that drifts over all drifted down over him.
At midnight he reached the end of his slumber,
And then he got up and said to his friend:

"Didn't you call me, my friend? What woke me up?
Didn't you touch me? What startled me?
Did a spirit pass over me? Why am I cold and numb?
My friend, I have had a fifth dream!   *170*
It was full of foreboding, a dream murky and grim.
I had just taken hold of a wild bull
That was bellowing and pawing the ground,
Raising clouds of dust that swirled up to the sky.
As I leaned into it my arms became tangled
In the bull's horns, but someone strong freed me
And gave me water to drink from his water-skin."

Enkidu told Gilgamesh what his dream meant:

"The monster we are going against, my friend,
Is not like that wild bull but completely different.   *180*
The wild bull in your dream was Shamash the Sun,
Who will take hold of our hands when we are in peril.
The one who gave you water from his water-skin
Was your guiding spirit, the god Lugalbanda.
We will join together and accomplish something
That has never been done before in this land."

W hen they were very close to the Cedar Forest
Enkidu saw Gilgamesh weeping and said:

"Why are tears flowing down your cheeks,
My friend? You are sprung from Uruk.   *190*
You must stand and fight, King Gilgamesh!"

Shamash heard all that had been spoken,
And now his voice cried out from the sky:

"Hurry, stand against him now! You must not allow
Humbaba to enter his forest, go down to his grove,
Must not let him put on all his seven cloaks!

He is wrapped in one now, six are still off.
They will make him stronger than a raging bull."

Then Humbaba bellowed, one long bellow,
A terrifying roar.   *200*
The keeper of the Cedar Forest bellowed,
Humbaba thundering like the Storm God himself.

Then Enkidu said to Gilgamesh:

"My strength is failing, my arms are weak and stiff."

Gilgamesh opened his mouth and said:

"Why are we talking like weaklings, my friend?
Didn't we cross all of those mountains?
Have not enemies in the past fallen before us?
We are experienced in combat, Enkidu,
Battle-hardened. Get rid of your fear.   *210*
Let your shout boom out like a kettle-drum!
Relax your arms, stop your knees from shaking.
Hand in hand, my friend, we will go on together.
Fix your mind completely on combat.
Forget about death and just go after life!
Whoever's out front watches out for both
And leads his comrade to safety.
Men like that make a name that lives on."

When they arrived at the distant forest's edge,
They stopped talking and came to a halt.   *220*

TABLET V

The Fight with Humbaba

There they stood, wondering at the forest,
Lifting their eyes to the towering cedars
And then staring into the forest's entrance.
They could see where Humbaba had worn a track,
A well-trodden path in and out of the woods.
They gazed at Cedar Mountain, throne of the gods,
Seat of goddesses, its great expanse
Shrouded with cool and fragrant shade,
The trees tangled with thickets of thorn
Under an arching canopy. Cedar saplings   *10*
Grew around the perimeter one league deep,
And cypresses for another two-thirds of a league.
The cedar bark was scabby with resin
Up to sixty cubits high, and the oozing sap
Dribbled down like raindrops into ravines.
Birds began to sing throughout the forest,
Answering each other, a constant din.
Cicadas joined in, chirping in chorus.
A wood pigeon moaned, a turtle dove called back.
The cries of storks and of francolins   *20*
Made the forest exult, the woodland rejoice.
Monkey mothers were crooning, and their young

Shrieked in unison. It was like a band of musicians
Beating out rhythms every day for Humbaba.

The cedars' shade filled Gilgamesh with terror.
His arms grew numb, and his legs weakened.
Enkidu opened his mouth and said to him:

"Let's move on to the heart of the forest,
Get to it and raise our battle-cry."
                                    And Gilgamesh:

Why are we trembling like cowards, my friend?   *30*
Didn't we cross all those mountains?
Aren't we going to pull through, see daylight again?"

And Enkidu answered:
                    "My friend,
You've seen combat before. Battle-hardened heroes
Have no fear of death. You've been soaked in blood;
You've got nothing to fear. Get mad now,
Whip yourself up into a frenzy now! Shake out
Your arms, feel the strength in your legs!"

Gilgamesh responded:
                    "Hold onto me,
My friend, and we will go ahead as one.   *40*
Keep your mind and heart fixed on combat."

The two heroes readied their weapons,
Pulled their swords from their scabbards,
And moved stealthily into Humbaba's lair.

Humbaba saw them coming and said to himself:

"Why are these two disturbing my land?
Surely Enkidu comes here in good will.
May Enlil curse him if he does not."

Enkidu and Gilgamesh pressed on,
Encouraging each other with words such as these: *50*

"Climbers in tandem can overcome
Even the steepest slope." And, "Two lion cubs
Can conquer even the mightiest lion."

But then they lost heart, Gilgamesh saying,

"We have come to a place where men should not go.
Let's just set our weapons in Humbaba's gate."

And Enkidu said to his friend in turn:

"Humbaba is ferocious, a hurricane wind;
He will mow us down like the Storm God himself.
Pray to Shamash to give us the thirteen winds!"   *60*

So Gilgamesh lifted his head up to Shamash,
His tears glistening in the rays of the sun:

"Hear me, O Shamash! If ever I have trusted you
Remember it now, and come to the aid
Of Gilgamesh, scion of Uruk!"

Shamash heard his prayer, and a voice
Shot down from the sky, saying:

"Do not be afraid. Stand up to Humbaba.
Do not let him go into the grove
And cloak himself in all his seven auras.   *70*
He is wrapped in only one of his auras now."

Then Humbaba bellowed, one terrifying bellow
Like a wild bull preparing to charge.
And they were face to face with the monster,
Whose mouth opened as he said to them:

"Only fools befriend brutish beasts, Gilgamesh.
Why have you come to stand before me?
And you, Enkidu, are a fish's spawn
Who knew no father, a turtle's hatchling
Who sucked at no mother's breast. I watched you   *80*
When you were little, but never came near you.
You wouldn't have made much of a meal for me.
And now you slyly bring Gilgamesh here,
And stand before me like an enemy, Enkidu.
I will slit Gilgamesh's gullet open
And feed his flesh to the vultures and hawks!"

Gilgamesh turned to Enkidu and said:

"O my friend, Humbaba looks different now!
We were bold in coming to his lair to defeat him,
But my heart is beating fast now."   *90*

Enkidu answered:

"Why are you talking like a coward, my friend?
Your gutless words are making me lose hope.
There's only one thing, my friend, for us to do now.
Strike while the iron is hot!
Let loose the flood! Crack the whip!
This is no time to hold back, to retreat.
Hit him hard, Gilgamesh!"

Gilgamesh and Humbaba squared off on each other,
And then the earth cracked open beneath their feet.   *100*
Mount Sirion and Lebanon reeled and shattered,
The white clouds turned black
And rained down a deathly mist upon them.
Shamash unleashed on Humbaba the mighty winds—
Winds from the South, the North, the East, and the West,
Colliding typhoons, cyclones, squalls, hurricanes, tempests,
Tornadoes and gales, twisters and whirlwinds—

Thirteen winds darkened Humbaba's face.
He could not move forward, could not pull back,
And Gilgamesh's weapons were now at his throat.   *110*
Humbaba pleaded with him for his life:
"You are so young, Gilgamesh, a mere child,
But truly the son of Wild Cow Ninsun!
You smashed the mountains at Shamash's command,
O offshoot of Uruk, Gilgamesh the King!
O Gilgamesh, a dead man is no use to his king.
Spare my life, lord, and allow me to live,
To dwell here for you in the Cedar Forest.
I will guard your trees and supply to you
As many as you want, cedar and myrtle,   *120*
Timber that will be the pride of your palace."

Enkidu opened his mouth and said to Gilgamesh:

"Do not listen, my friend, to what Humbaba says,
Ignore his entreaties."

                    Then Humbaba said to Enkidu:

"You know the ways of the wild, and you also know
The art of speech. I should have strung you up
From a sapling at the forest's entrance,
Should have fed your flesh to the vultures and hawks.
But now, Enkidu, my salvation lies with you.
Tell Gilgamesh to spare my life."   *130*

But Enkidu said this to Gilgamesh:

"Finish him off, my friend, destroy this Humbaba
Who guards the Cedar Forest, end his power,
Before supreme Enlil hears of what we do.
The great gods will turn their wrath against us,
Enlil in Nippur, Shamash in Larsa.

Make a name for yourself that will endure forever,
Gilgamesh who killed the ferocious Humbaba!"

Humbaba heard Enkidu. He lifted his head and said:

"You sit by him like a shepherd, like his servant.   *140*
My salvation lies with you, Enkidu.
Tell Gilgamesh to spare my life."

But Enkidu said this to Gilgamesh:

"Finish him off, my friend, destroy this Humbaba
Who guards the Cedar Forest, end his power,
Before supreme Enlil hears of what we do.
The great gods will turn their wrath against us,
Enlil in Nippur, Shamash in Larsa.
Make a name for yourself that will endure forever,
Gilgamesh who killed the ferocious Humbaba!"   *150*

When Humbaba heard this he cursed them both:

"May the two of you never grow old together,
And may no one but Gilgamesh bury Enkidu."

Then Enkidu said to Gilgamesh:

"I speak to you, but you aren't listening, my friend.
As for these curses, may they fly back to his mouth."

Gilgamesh heard his friend. He pulled out
The long dagger that hung from his belt
And struck Humbaba deep in the neck.
Enkidu helped him to pull out his lungs,   *160*
And then Gilgamesh leapt up
And cut the tusks from his jaws as a trophy.

A heavy rain began to fall on the mountain,
And the rain kept falling, falling on the mountain.

Gilgamesh and Enkidu then pulled out
Their heavy axes and began to cut timber.
The woodchips flew, three cubits long each,
As they picked out and felled all the best trees.

Then Enkidu said to Gilgamesh:

"My friend, this lofty cedar we just now cut,   *170*
Whose crest towered up to the heavens,
We will make a door from it, a great door
Six rods high, two rods wide, and a cubit thick,
Pole and both pivots all from one solid piece.
The Euphrates River will carry it downstream
To Enlil's temple, his sanctuary in Nippur,
And all of the people will rejoice in this door."

The two heroes lashed together a raft
And loaded onto it all the cedar they had cut.
Enkidu poled the raft, and Gilgamesh   *180*
Carried Humbaba's severed head.

TABLET VI

The Bull of Heaven

When they were back in Uruk, Gilgamesh
Washed his matted hair and wiped down his gear.
He shook his hair out over his shoulders,
Then, putting on fresh, clean clothes,
He cinched his robes with a sash and put on his crown.

He was beautiful to see, and the goddess Ishtar
Looked at him with desire. She said to him:

"Come, my Gilgamesh, and marry me.
Grant me your fruits, O please, grant them.
Be my husband, and I'll be your wife. *10*
I will rig you a chariot of lapis lazuli and gold,
With golden wheels and yoke-horns of amber.
You will drive a team of lions flanked by great mules
As you enter our cedar-scented house,
And as you enter, the doorway and exotic foot-stool
Will kiss your feet! Kings and courtiers
Will kneel before you, bringing as tribute
All that the mountains and plains produce,
Your goats will bear triplets, your ewes twins,
Your laden donkey will outrun any mule, *20*

Your team of horses will gallop in glory,
No ox will be a match for yours at the yoke."

Gilgamesh answered the Lady Ishtar this way:

"If I do marry you, how will you take care of me?
How will you clothe me, what food will I have?
Will you bring me bread that is fit for a god,
Pour me ale fit for king? Who would marry you?
You are frost and ice, a drafty door,
A palace that slaughters its warriors,
A rogue elephant, pitch that stains the hands,   *30*
A waterskin that wearies its bearer,
Limestone that weakens an ashlar wall.
You are a wall-shattering battering ram,
A shoe that cramps the foot it is on.
Let me tell the tale of your lovers. First,
Dumuzi, whom you loved when you were young.
You doomed him to unending lamenting.
Next you loved the dappled Allallu Bird,
And then attacked him and broke his wing.
Now he cries 'My wing!' on the forest floor.   *40*
You loved the lion, that paragon of strength,
But then dug seven times seven pits to entrap him.
You loved the noble horse, renowned in battle,
But then destined him to the whip and spur,
Destined him to twenty-mile gallops,
Destined him to drink from muddy pools,
Dooming his mother Silili to constant weeping.
You loved the herdsman, who grazes his flocks.
He brought you loaves of ember-baked bread,
He butchered kids for you every single day.   *50*
With one blow you turned him into a wolf,
And now his own herders chase him away,
His own dogs snap at their master's buttocks.
You loved your father's gardener, loved Ishullanu,

Who used to bring you baskets of dates
So that your table glistened with fruit every day.
You had your eye on him and sidled up, saying,
'Ishullanu, let's have a taste of your zest.
Put your hand down here and rub my clit.'
But Ishullanu answered you,   *60*
'Me? Why are you bothering with me?
Didn't my mother bake bread? Am I so hungry
That I have to eat abuse and lies?
Should I sleep under only rushes in winter?'
When you heard what Ishullanu said
You hit him and turned him into a dwarf
And sat him down in the garden to work
Where he can never get up or ever lie down.
Must you love me too, and treat me like this?"

Ishtar listened to what Gilgamesh said   *70*
And then flew up to heaven, raging mad.
In tears she went to her father Anu
And to Antu her mother, and poured out her heart:

"Father Anu, Gilgamesh keeps scorning me
And slandering me with obscene stories.
I am insulted!"

                    Anu said to his daughter:

"But didn't you provoke King Gilgamesh
Into telling these slanderous stories about you
And insulting you?"

                    Ishtar answered him:

"Father, give me the Bull of Heaven, please,   *80*
So I can kill Gilgamesh at home in Uruk.
And if you do not give me the Bull of Heaven

I will smash open the gates of the Underworld
And free all the dead from their dwelling below.
I will make the dead rise and devour the living,
And then the dead will outnumber the living."

Anu then said to his daughter Ishtar:

"If you want me to give you the Bull of Heaven,
Uruk's widows must gather chaff seven years,
And Uruk's farmers grow seven years of hay."   *90*

And Ishtar said to her father Anu:

"I have already accomplished all this.
Uruk's widows have gathered chaff seven years,
And Uruk's farmers have grown seven years of hay.
I shall have my vengeance with the Bull's raging fury."

When Anu heard Ishtar say this, he handed to her
The tether to the nose-ring of the Bull of Heaven.
Ishtar led him down, led him all the way
To the land of Uruk. The Bull dried up the woods
And surrounding marshes, left the wetlands dry   *100*
And then went to the river, lowering its level
By no less than twelve feet. Then the Bull snorted
And a pit opened up, swallowing a hundred men.
The Bull snorted again and a second pit opened,
Into which two hundred of Uruk's men fell.
The third time the Bull of Heaven snorted
Another pit opened, and Enkidu fell in
Up to his waist. But then Enkidu leaped up
Out of the pit and took the Bull by his horns.
The Bull snorted sputum into his face,   *110*
And Enkidu cried out to Gilgamesh, saying:

"We flaunted our deeds in the city, my friend.
How are we going to look to the people now?

My friend, I've tested this Bull's strength,
And have some idea of its might and temper.
Let me test it again, from behind this time.
I'm going to grab it by the tail and set my foot
In the back of his leg. You'll have to be like
A brave, skillful butcher and drive your knife
Into the sweet spot between his two horns." 120

Enkidu got back quickly behind the Bull
Grabbed it by the tail and planted his foot
In the back of his leg. And Gilgamesh,
Like a brave, skillful butcher, drove his knife
Into the sweet spot between the Bull's horns.

After they had killed the Bull of Heaven
Gilgamesh and Enkidu bore its heart
Up to Shamash and set it down before him.
They stepped back and prostrated themselves
In the presence of the Sun God, and then sat down. 130
Ishtar had gone up onto Uruk's wall
And was stamping her feet. She wailed aloud:

"Oh, Gilgamesh mocked me and now he has killed
The Bull of Heaven!"

Enkidu heard this,
And tearing a haunch off the Bull
He hurled it at the goddess, saying:

"If I had caught you I'd have treated you the same
And plastered his guts all over your body!"

Ishtar convened the courtesans and prostitutes
To mourn over the haunch of the Bull of Heaven, 140
While Gilgamesh summoned the smiths and artisans.
They were stunned at the size of the horns,
A mass of lapis lazuli worth thirty minas,

Each rim worth another two minas,
And together they held six barrels of oil.
He dedicated the horns to his god, Lugalbanda,
To hold oil for anointing,
Took them inside to hang in the god's chamber.

They washed their hands in the Euphrates
And walked back hand in hand.   *150*
When they drove their chariot through Uruk's streets
The whole city came out to look at them.
Back in his palace Gilgamesh asked the serving girls:

"Who is most glorious, the most glorious of men?"

And the response came back:

"Gilgamesh is most glorious, the most glorious of men!"

And so Gilgamesh celebrated in his palace.

That night all the men were asleep in their beds,
And Enkidu had a dream while he slept.

TABLET VII

The Death of Enkidu

Dawn.

Enkidu rose to tell Gilgamesh his dream.

"My friend, why were the great gods in council?
O, my friend, what a dream I had last night!
The gods were in an assembly, Anu, Enlil,
Ea, and Shamash the Sun. Anu said to Enlil:
'These two slaughtered the Bull of Heaven,
And they killed Humbaba who guarded the cedar.
So one of them,' said Anu, 'has to die.'
Then Enlil said, 'Enkidu must die,   10
Not Gilgamesh.' Then Shamash replied to Enlil:
'Didn't I tell them to kill the Bull of Heaven
And Humbaba too? Didn't they kill them at my behest?
And now innocent Enkidu must die?'
Then Enlil grew angry with Shamash the Sun:
'And you were their companion every single day!'"

Then Enkidu lay down before Gilgamesh,
Weeping and lamenting.
                              "O my brother,

My dear, dear brother. They will never again
Raise me up for my brother. No, I will sit   *20*
Among the dead, I will cross the threshold
Of the dead, never see my dear brother again."

When dawn broke, Enkidu lifted his eyes
To the doorway, and he said to the door:

"You cannot hear me, Door from the woods.
I can hear and understand, but you cannot.
I searched twenty leagues to find timber for you
Until I found in the forest a fine, tall cedar,
The finest tree in the whole Cedar Forest.
You are six rods high, two rods in width,   *30*
And a cubit thick. Your axle and pivots
Are all one piece, from top to bottom.
I built you, I lifted you, I hung you in Nippur.
If I had known, Door, you would reward me like this,
I would have swung my axe and cut you down,
Floated you downstream to Ebabbara,
Shamash's temple in Sippar, set you up there
As a cedar door in the glorious temple
And set up a thunderbird in the gateway,
Because Shamash heard my prayer   *40*
And gave me a weapon in a time of peril.
I was the one who built you, who lifted you up.
So why could I not tear you down now?
May a king who comes after me hate you, Door,
Or hang you somewhere else, or may he
Remove my name and put his own name on you."

As Enkidu listened to his own words, his tears
Began to flow, and as Gilgamesh listened
To the words of his friend Enkidu
Gilgamesh's tears began to flow too.   *50*
He opened his mouth and said to his friend:

"Ah, my noble friend, why do you, whose mind
Was once so sound, now speak so profanely?
Your dream was not an ordinary dream.
Your mind is troubled, buzzing with anxiety.
This was a strange, most unusual dream.
When someone has a dream like this
Only grief is left to the one who survives.
I will pray to the great gods, beseech them,
Shamash especially. I will beseech your god.   60
And I will pray to Anu, the father of the gods.
May Enlil hear me as I pray in your presence.
I will shape a statue of you out of pure gold."

"No, my friend, offer no silver, no gold.
Enlil's words are not like the other gods'.
What he commands he does not rub out,
Does not rub out the decrees he sets down.
My fate is fixed, my friend.
People do go to their doom before their time."

When dawn's first light appeared in the sky   70
Enkidu lifted his head toward Shamash and cried,
His tears glistening in the rays of the sun:

"I beg you, Shamash, to spare my dear life.
But that hunter, the trapper, the man
Who stopped me from being as great as my friend,
May that hunter never be as great as his friend!
May he lose his property and be left destitute,
May the god in his house fly out the window!"

When he had enough of cursing the hunter,
He began to curse the harlot Shamhat as well: 80

"And now, Shamhat, I will fix your fate,
Your perpetual doom! My mighty curse

Will afflict you now and forevermore.
May you never have a home to give you joy,
Never have a family to live with,
Never sit among the young women in their quarters.
May a drunkard puke on your fancy gown,
May you never have any beautiful things,
No lovely pottery, no banquet table
For people to set with a sumptuous feast,   90
No bed to enjoy but a miserable board.
May you squat at the crossroads, sleep
In the fields, stand in the shadow of a wall,
The soles of your feet raw from briars and thorns.
May men drunk and sober slap your face.
May angry wives file lawsuits against you.
May no builder ever plaster your ceiling.
May owls roost in the rafters of your house,
And no banquet ever grace your table.

"And this is all because you made me weak   100
When I was natural and pure, weakened me
When I was pure and natural in the wilderness."

Shamash heard what Enkidu was saying,
And a great voice boomed down from the sky:

"Enkidu, why are you cursing the harlot Shamhat?
She served you bread that was fit for a god,
Poured you ale that was fit for a king,
Clothed you in resplendent garments,
And matched you with handsome Gilgamesh.
And now Gilgamesh, your friend and brother,   110
Will lay you out on a magnificent bed,
A bed of honor, and place you on his left.
The underworld lords will all kiss your feet.
He will have all Uruk lament and mourn you,
Fill all the city's people full of grief for you.

And when you are gone his hair will be matted,
Clad in a lion skin he will wander the wild."

Enkidu heard the words of great Shamash.
The anger in his heart subsided,
His furious heart grew calm, and he said: *120*

"Come, Shamhat, and I will pronounce your fate.
The mouth that cursed you can bless you as well.
Rulers and nobles will be your lovers.
At one league off, men will slap their thighs,
And at two leagues they will shake out their hair!
No warrior will delay to drop his belt for you.
They will give you obsidian and lapis lazuli,
Golden earrings and jewels. Ishtar herself,
The most gifted of gods, will usher you in
To the wealthiest houses. Rich men will desert   *130*
Even their wives who have borne seven sons."

But Enkidu's mind was still troubled.
He lay alone on his bed, deep in thought,
And then told Gilgamesh what was on his mind:

"My friend, what a dream I had last night!
The sky thundered, the earth echoed the sound,
And I was standing there between heaven and earth
Alongside a man with a terrifying face,
As grim and frightening as a Thunderbird's.
His hands were like the paws of a lion,   *140*
But with claws like the talons of an eagle,
And he seized me by the hair, overpowering me.
I hit him, but he struck back with the force
Of a snapping whip and keeled me over,
Crushing me underfoot like a great wild bull
And drenching me with his poisonous slaver.
I cried out to you, 'Help me my friend!'

You were afraid, but still . . .

. . . and then he turned me into a dove,

Binding my arms like the wings of a bird.   *150*

He led me down to the House of Darkness,

Irkalla's abode, the house no one leaves,

Led me down the path that has no return.

Those who stay there are deprived of light,

They have no food but soil, eat only clay,

And are clad in coats of feathers like birds,

Dwelling in the dark and lightless gloom.

Dust lay thick on the door.

It was a House of Dust, steeped in death's quiet,

A House of Dust that I entered.   *160*

Around me I saw a crowd of crowned heads

Who had ruled the land in ancient times,

Served the roast at the table of Anu, of Enlil,

Served them baked bread, poured them cool water.

And there were priests in the House of Dust,

Priests for all the offerings and rites,

Priests of the great gods.

Etana was there, and Shakkan,

And the goddess Ereshkigal, Queen of the Underworld,

And sitting by her Belet-seri, the Underworld's scribe,   *170*

Reading aloud from a tablet she held.

She lifted her head when she saw me

And said, 'Who brought this man here?'"

"I went through so much with you, my friend.

Remember me. Never forget what I did."

And Gilgamesh:

               "What a vision my friend has had!"

Enkidu was exhausted all the rest of that day.

He lay in bed all day sick and disheartened.

The next day he was worse. A third day passed,

And a fourth. His sickness grew worse each day.   *180*
On the twelfth day Enkidu called from his bed
For Gilgamesh, and he said to his friend:

"My god has turned against me, my friend.
I am dying, but not like one who falls in combat,
Not like that. I will not make a name for myself
The way I am dying, not make a name . . ."

TABLET VIII

Enkidu's Funeral

Dawn's first light was just brightening the sky
When Gilgamesh began to lament his friend:

"O Enkidu, a gazelle was your mother
And your father a wild donkey.
You were reared on the milk of wild asses,
And the beasts of the wild showed you the pastures.

O Enkidu, may the trails in the Cedar Forest
Never cease to mourn you, by day and by night.

May the elders of thronging Uruk lament you,
May the crowds who cheered for us mourn you.   *10*

May the high hills and mountains mourn you.
May the pastures mourn for you like your mother.

May the cypress and cedar lament you,
All the trees we wound through in our fury!

May the bear, the hyena, the leopard, and lion lament you,
The wild bull, the deer, all the beasts of the forest.

May the sacred river Ulay mourn for you,
Along whose banks we strode in our strength.

May the unsullied Euphrates lament you,
Whose water we poured from skins in libation. *20*

May the young men of Uruk mourn you,
Who watched us battle the Bull of Heaven!

May the plowman in his field lament you
As he trills your name up and down the furrows.

May the shepherd lament you in the pasture,
Who made the milk and butter sweet for your mouth.

May the shepherd boy weep for you,
Who brought the ghee to your lips.

May the brew-master mourn you,
Who brewed ale for you to drink. *30*

May the harlot lament you,
Who anointed you with fragrant oil.

May all the women in the house mourn you,
May they mourn you like a brother,
May they let their hair lie loose on their backs
As if they were your sisters.

May they all do this for you, Enkidu,
And on this very day I, too, will mourn you.
Hear me, O young men of Uruk,
Hear me, O elders! *40*
I will weep for my friend Enkidu,
Will wail bitterly like a woman who mourns.

He was the trusted axe at my side,
The dagger in my belt, the shield before me,
My festive robe, the sash I loved to wear,
And an evil wind has swept it all away.

O my friend, highland donkey, leopard in the wild
O my friend Enkidu, a wild ass stampeding,
We teamed up together, climbed high mountains,
Took hold of the Bull of Heaven and killed him,   *50*
And destroyed Humbaba in the Cedar Forest!

What is this sleep that has seized you now?
Are you unconscious, and do you not hear me?"

But Enkidu did not respond, did not lift his head.
Gilgamesh felt his heart, but it was no longer beating.
He veiled his friend's face as if it were his bride's,
And circled him like an eagle, paced to and fro
Like a lioness who has lost her cubs.
He tore out clumps of his curly hair
And ripped off his fine robes as if they were cursed.   *60*
When dawn's first glimmer appeared in the sky,
Gilgamesh called out to all his people:

"Forge-master, coppersmith, goldsmith, jeweler,
Fashion a statue of my friend!"

Then he said to Enkidu:

"Your eyebrows will be lapis lazuli, your chest gold.
I will lay you out on a royal bed,
You will lie on my left, in a place of honor.
The lords of the underworld will kiss your feet."

Then Gilgamesh unsealed his treasury   *70*
And inspected his precious gems and stones,

Lapis lazuli, carnelian, obsidian, alabaster.
These he provided for his friend,
Along with many minas of gold
And many talents of ivory,
And a golden axe with an ivory handle
Three cubits in length,
And a golden bow and quiver of arrows.

He butchered fattened oxen and sheep for his friend
And carried the meat to the underworld's lords.   *80*

He brought a staff of polished, gleaming wood
As a gift for Ishtar, and showed it to the Sun God:
"May Ishtar the great Queen accept this gift,
May she welcome my friend and walk at his side."

He brought a flask of lapis lazuli
For Ereshkigal, and showed it to the Sun God:
"May Ereshkigal, the Underworld Queen, accept this,
May she welcome my friend and walk at his side."

He brought a carnelian flute for Dumuzi,
Ishtar's beloved shepherd, and showed it to the Sun God: *90*
"May Dumuzi, Ishtar's beloved shepherd, accept this,
May he welcome my friend and walk at his side."

He brought a lapis lazuli chair and staff for Namtar,
Minister of the Underworld, and showed it to the Sun God:
"May Namtar, Minister of the Underworld, accept this,
May he welcome my friend and walk at his side."

He brought a gift also for Hushbisha, who serves
In the Underworld and showed it to the Sun God:
"May Hushbisha, who serves in the Underworld, accept this,
May she welcome my friend and walk at his side."   *100*

And he brought silver for Qassu-tabat,
Ereshkigal's sweeper, and showed it to the Sun God:
"May Qassu-tabat, Ereshkigal's sweeper, accept this,
May she welcome my friend and walk at his side.
May my friend not languish or be sick at heart."

And an alabaster bowl inlaid with carnelian
And lapis lazuli, depicting the Cedar Forest,
He brought for Ninshuluhhatumma, who cleans
The house of the dead, and showed it to the Sun God:
"May Ninshuluhhatumma accept this,   *110*
May she welcome my friend and walk at his side.
May my friend not languish or be sick at heart."

And a two-edged dagger with a lapis lazuli haft,
Etched with an image of the pure Euphrates,
He brought for Bibbu, the Underworld's butcher,
And he showed it to the Sun God:
"May the butcher of the teeming Underworld accept this,
May he welcome my friend and walk at his side."

And he brought a chair with an alabaster back
For Dumuzi-abzu, the Underworld's scapegoat,   *120*
And he showed it to the Sun God:
"May Dumuzi-abzu, the Underworld's scapegoat accept this.
May he welcome my friend and walk at his side."

When dawn's first glimmers appeared in the sky
Gilgamesh opened the palace gate.
He brought out a great table of polished wood
And filled a carnelian dish with honey
And one of lapis lazuli with ghee.
All this he adorned and presented to the Sun.

TABLET IX

The Quest for Immortality

Gilgamesh shed bitter tears for his friend Enkidu.
Wandering through wild lands he said to himself:

"Will I not die someday and be just like Enkidu?
My heart is pierced through with sorrow!
I am afraid of death, and so I wander the wild
Searching for Utanapishtim, son of Ubar-Tutu.
Moving swiftly along, I came one night
To a mountain pass and saw a pride of lions.
I was afraid and lifted my head in prayer
To Sin, the moon, lamp of the gods,   *10*
Praying to him to keep me from harm."

He lay down then and later woke from a dream
Under the moonlight, filled with the joy of life.
He picked up his axe, drew his dagger from his belt,
And fell like an arrow upon the lions,
Killing some of them and scattering the rest.

Clad now in their skins and eating their flesh,
Gilgamesh dug new wells wherever he went
And drank their water as he chased the wind.

Shamash the Sun was concerned   *20*
And leaning low said to Gilgamesh:

"Where are you wandering, Gilgamesh?
You will never find the life you are seeking."

And Gilgamesh answered the great Shamash:

"After I wander this whole, wild world
Will I lack rest down in the world below?
No, I will lie there asleep age after age.
Let my eyes now be filled with sunlight.
Will there be any light in the hidden dark?
Do the dead ever see the sun's shining rays?"   *30*

He came to the twin mountains of Mashu
That guard the daily rising of the sun.
Their peaks support the tent of the sky,
Their roots stretch down to the Underworld.
Guarding the gate there were the Scorpion People,
Terrible beings whose very glance was death,
Whose fearsome radiance engulfed the mountains.
They guarded the sun at its rising and setting.

When Gilgamesh saw them he covered his face
In awe and dread, but then gathered his courage   *40*
And approached them. One of the Scorpion People
Said to his mate, "This man has the flesh of the gods."
His mate answered, "Two parts god, one part human."
The Scorpion Man called out to Gilgamesh,
Gilgamesh the king, the flesh of the gods:

"How have you travelled so far a road?
How have you come to stand here before me?
How did you cross the perilous seas?
Tell me of your journey. Where are you headed?"

Gilgamesh answered:

"I seek the road to my ancestor Utanapishtim,   *50*
Who found eternal life at the gods' assembly.
He will tell me the secret of life and death."

And the Scorpion Man said to Gilgamesh:

"There has never been anyone like you, Gilgamesh.
No one has ever travelled the path through this mountain.
It takes twelve double-hours to pass through inside.
The darkness is dense, and there is no light at all,
Neither after sunrise nor after sunset.
No one has done it. How will you do it?"

Gilgamesh said:

"I have come through sorrow,   *60*
My face is burnt by frost and sunlight,
Come through fatigue . . ."

And the Scorpion Man said to Gilgamesh,
Gilgamesh the king, the flesh of the gods:

"Go, Gilgamesh!
May you pass through the mountain of Mashu.
May the hills and mountains protect you,
May they keep you safe on your journey,
May the gate of the mountains be open for you."

Gilgamesh heard what the Scorpion Man said   *70*
And set out on the road of the Sun God.

At the first double hour
The darkness was dense; there was no light at all.
He could not see anything behind him.

At the second double hour
The darkness was dense; there was no light at all.
He could not see anything behind him.

At the third double hour
The darkness was dense; there was no light at all.
He could not see anything behind him.　　　　　　　　　*80*

At the fourth double hour
The darkness was dense; there was no light at all.
He could not see anything behind him.

At the fifth double hour
The darkness was dense; there was no light at all.
He could not see anything behind him.

At the sixth double hour
The darkness was dense; there was no light at all.
He could not see anything behind him.

At the seventh double hour　　　　　　　　　*90*
The darkness was dense; there was no light at all.
He could not see anything behind him.

At the eighth double hour
The darkness was dense; there was no light at all.
He could not see anything behind him.

At the ninth double hour
He felt the north wind in his face,
But the darkness was dense; there was no light at all.
He could not see anything behind him.

When he reached the tenth double hour　　　　　　　　　*100*
He was nearing the end.

When he reached the eleventh double hour
There was only a journey of one double hour left.

When he reached the twelfth double hour
Gilgamesh came out before the sun did.

The light was brilliant.
He saw trees and went straight to them,
The trees of the gods.
A carnelian tree was heavy with fruit,
Bunches of grapes, a beautiful sight.   *110*

A tree with lapis lazuli leaves,
The fruit on its limbs lovely to see.

There was cypress, cedar,
Leaf stems of exotic stone,
Sea-coral,
              stone vials instead of thorns.
He touched a carob,
                    it was agate.

And as Gilgamesh walked around there
A woman lifted her head to watch him.   *120*

TABLET X

Shiduri's Tavern

Shiduri lived by the shore of the sea
Where she had an inn and a tavern
With racks of pots and golden vats.
Wrapped in shawls and with her face veiled,
She saw Gilgamesh come wandering up
Clad in pelts, a fearful sight.
His body's flesh was the flesh of gods,
But his heart was filled with sorrow.
He looked like one who had come a long way.
As the tavern-keeper watched from a distance,   *10*
Thinking it over, she said to herself:

"This man has to be a hunter of bulls,
But where is he from, coming straight for my gate?"

Seeing him like this, she barred her gate,
Barred her gate and climbed up to her roof.
Gilgamesh heard something. He lifted his chin,
Turned, and said to the tavern-keeper:

"Why did you bar your gate, tavern-keeper,
As soon as you saw me? You barred your gate
And got up on your roof. I'll knock down your door!"   *20*

And Shiduri shot back to Gilgamesh:

"So I barred my gate and went up on the roof.
You have to tell me about your journey."

Then Gilgamesh said to the tavern-keeper:

"My friend Enkidu and I, we teamed up,
We climbed mountains, we caught and killed
The Bull of Heaven, killed Humbaba too
In the Cedar Forest, and lions up in the high passes."

Shiduri the tavern-keeper responded:

"If you were the ones who killed Humbaba,   30
Killed the guardian of the Cedar Forest,
And lions up in the mountain passes,
And who caught and killed the Bull of Heaven,
Why are your eyes so sunken, your cheeks hollow?
Why are you so sorrowful and look so bad,
Like someone who comes from far away,
Your skin sunburnt, your face frost-bitten?
And why do you wander the wild in lion skins?"

And Gilgamesh said to the tavern-keeper:

"Should my eyes not be sunken, my cheeks hollow?   40
Should I not be sorrowful and look so bad,
Like someone who comes from far away,
My skin sunburnt and my face frostbitten?
Should I not wander the wilderness in lion skins?
My friend, who was like a wild ass on the run,
An upland donkey, a leopard in the wild,
My friend Enkidu, a wild ass on the run,
An upland donkey, a leopard in the wild,
My beloved friend, so dear to me,

Who was with me in every peril,   *50*
My friend Enkidu, whom I loved so much,
Who was with me in every peril,
Death has overtaken him, the doom of mortals.
Six days and seven nights I mourned for him
And did not give up his body for burial
Until maggots were crawling out of his nostrils.
Then I became afraid that I would die too,
Terrified of death, and so I wander the wild.
What happened to my friend was too much for me,
And so I wander far, wander far in the wild.   *60*
What happened to Enkidu was too much for me,
And so I wander far, wander far in the wild.
How can I sit quietly, doing nothing?
I loved my friend and he has turned into clay,
My beloved Enkidu has turned into clay.
Will I not be like him? Will I not lie down too
And never rise again, lie down forever?"

Gilgamesh paused, and then asked Shiduri:

"And now, tavern-keeper, where is the road
To Utanapishtim? Where does it start?   *70*
Tell me how to find it. Tell me!
If there is a way, I will cross the ocean,
If there is not, I will wander the wild."

And Shiduri the tavern-keeper:

"O Gilgamesh, there is no way to cross it,
No one has ever crossed the ocean.
Only great Shamash crosses the ocean.
Besides the Sun God who could ever cross it?
It is a perilous crossing, full of danger,
Blocked in the middle by the Waters of Death.   *80*
Even if you cross the ocean that far, Gilgamesh,

What will you do when you reach the Waters of Death?
But over there, Gilgamesh, is Utanapishtim's boatman,
Urshanabi. With him are the Stone Ones
As he trims pines in the middle of the forest.
Go to see him, present yourself to him.
Go across with him, if there is a way,
And if not, turn around and come back."

As soon as Gilgamesh heard this
He picked up his axe and drew his dagger.   *90*
He crept forward and then charged down,
Falling on them like an arrow from a bow.
His voice boomed through the forest.
When Urshanabi saw the glint of a weapon
He took out an axe himself,
But Gilgamesh struck him on the head,
Seized his arm and pushed him aside.
The Stone Ones—who crewed the boat
And were immune to the Waters of Death—
Panicked and fled. Gilgamesh cut them off   *100*
On the Ocean's shore and in his relentless fury
Smashed them to pieces, which he threw into the water.
Then he returned and stood over Urshanabi,
Who looked Gilgamesh in the eye and said to him:

"Tell me your name. I am Urshanabi,
Boatman of Utanapishtim the Distant."

Gilgamesh said to Urshanabi:

"My name is Gilgamesh.
I have come from Uruk-Eanna
And found a way through the mountains,   *110*
The hidden road of the Sun."

Then Urshanabi said to Gilgamesh:

"Why are your eyes so sunken, your cheeks hollow?
Why are you so sorrowful and look so bad,
Like someone who comes from far away,
Your skin sunburnt, your face frost-bitten?
And why do you wander the wild in lion skins?"

And Gilgamesh said to Urshanabi the boatman:

"Should my eyes not be sunken, my cheeks hollow?
Should I not be sorrowful and look so bad   *120*
Like someone who comes from far away
My skin sunburnt and my face frostbitten?
Should I not wander the wild in lion skins?
My friend, who was like a wild ass on the run,
An upland donkey, a leopard in the wild,
My friend Enkidu, a wild ass on the run,
An upland donkey, a leopard in the wild—
My friend Enkidu, he and I teamed up,
We climbed mountains, we caught and killed
The Bull of Heaven, killed Humbaba too   *130*
In the Cedar Forest, and lions up in the high passes—
My beloved friend, so dear to me,
Who was with me in every peril,
My friend Enkidu, whom I loved so much,
Who was with me in every peril,
Death has overtaken him, the doom of mortals.
Six days and seven nights I mourned for him
And did not give up his body for burial
Until maggots were crawling in his nostrils.
Then I became afraid that I would die too,   *140*
Terrified of death, and so I wander the wild.
What happened to my friend was too much for me,
And so I wander far, wander far in the wild.
What happened to Enkidu was too much for me,
And so I wander far, wander far in the wild.
How can I sit quietly, doing nothing?

I loved my friend and he has turned into clay,
My beloved Enkidu has turned into clay.
Will I not be like him? Will I not lie down too
And never rise again, lie down forever?"   *150*

Gilgamesh paused, and then said to Urshanabi:

"And now, Urshanabi, boatman, show me the way
To Utanapishtim. Where does it start?
Tell me how to find it. Tell me!
If there is a way, I will cross the ocean,
If there is not, I will wander the wild."

Then Urshanabi said to Gilgamesh:

"Your own hands made your crossing impossible
When you smashed the Stone Ones, Gilgamesh.
The Stone Ones are smashed, the pine untrimmed.   *160*
Take your axe, Gilgamesh, and go down to the forest,
Cut three hundred punting-poles, each five rods long.
Trim them and put a boss on the end of each one,
Then bring them back here and show them to me."

Gilgamesh heard this. He picked up his axe,
Drew out his dagger and went down to the forest.
He cut three hundred punting-poles, each five rods long,
Trimmed them and put a boss on the end of each one,
And then brought them to Urshanabi the boatman.

Gilgamesh and Urshanabi manned the boat,   *170*
They launched it and crewed it all by themselves.
A month and a half journey they made in three days,
And when Urshanabi saw that they had reached
The Waters of Death, he called to Gilgamesh:

"Now, Gilgamesh! Take the first punting-pole,
And don't touch the water or your hand will wither.
Now a second punting-pole, Gilgamesh, a third, a fourth!
A fifth punting-pole, Gilgamesh, a sixth, a seventh!
An eighth punting-pole, Gilgamesh, a ninth, a tenth!
An eleventh punting-pole, Gilgamesh, and now a twelfth!"   180

At a hundred and twenty double furlongs
Gilgamesh had gone through all of the poles.
Urshanabi then took off his clothing,
And Gilgamesh did the same. Stretching out his arms
Gilgamesh made them into a yard-arm to rig up a sail.

Utanapishtim was watching all this from a distance,
And when he saw Gilgamesh he said to himself,
Trying to understand, turning it over in his mind:

"Why are the ship's Stone Ones all broken,
And who is this aboard, there on the right?   190
I am looking hard at him. He is not a pilot,
Not one of my men, this man in the boat."

When Gilgamesh was close to the dock
He hailed Utanapishtim, addressing him
As the hero who had survived the Deluge.

And Utanapishtim said to Gilgamesh:

"Why are your eyes so sunken, your cheeks hollow?
Why are you so sorrowful and look so bad,
Like someone who comes from far away,
Your skin sunburnt, your face frost-bitten?   200
And why do you wander the wild in lion skins?"

Then Gilgamesh said to Utanapishtim:

"Should my eyes not be sunken, my cheeks hollow?
Should I not be sorrowful and look so bad
Like someone who comes from far away
My skin sunburnt and my face frostbitten?
Should I not wander the wildnerness in lion skins?
My friend, who was like a wild ass on the run,
An upland donkey, a leopard in the wild,
My friend Enkidu, a wild ass on the run,   *210*
An upland donkey, a leopard in the wild—
My friend Enkidu, he and I teamed up,
We climbed mountains, we caught and killed
The Bull of Heaven, killed Humbaba too
In the Cedar Forest, and lions up in the high passes—
My beloved friend, so dear to me,
Who was with me in every peril,
My friend Enkidu, whom I loved so much,
Who was with me in every peril,
Death has overtaken him, the doom of mortals.   *220*
Six days and seven nights I mourned for him
And did not give up his body for burial
Until maggots were crawling in his nostrils.
Then I became afraid that I would die too,
Terrified of death, and so I wander the wild.
What happened to my friend was too much for me,
And so I wander far, wander far in the wild.
What happened to Enkidu was too much for me,
And so I wander far, wander far in the wild.
How can I sit quietly, doing nothing?   *230*
I loved my friend and he has turned into clay,
My beloved Enkidu has turned into clay.
Will I not be like him? Will I not lie down too
And never rise again, lie down forever?"

Gilgamesh paused, and then said to Utanapishtim:

"I said to myself, 'I have heard men talk about
 Utanapishtim the Distant. I will go find him.'
I climbed over many fearsome mountains,
Crossed all the seas and crossed them again.
My eyes were never closed for long in sweet sleep;   *240*
I ravaged my body by going without sleep.
Every vein in my body is filled with grief,
And what has it gotten me, all my hard trials?
My clothes were worn before I reached the tavern-keeper.
I killed bears, hyenas, lions and leopards,
Deer and ibex, all the beasts of the wild,
I ate their flesh, skinned them for their pelts.
May the gate of sorrow now be barred,
Sorrow's door sealed tight with tar and pitch.
They will no longer stop dancing because of me.   *250*
My people now will be happy for me."

Then Utanapishtim said to Gilgamesh:

"Why do you always pursue sorrow, Gilgamesh,
You whose flesh is both human and divine,
Made by the gods like your father and mother?
Have you ever compared yourself with a fool?
They put a throne in the assembly and told you to sit.
The fool gets leftovers instead of fresh ghee,
Bran and chaff instead of fine flour.
He wears rags instead of nice clothes,   *260*
Rags held up by a rope instead of a belt.
He has no counselors to give him advice,
So all his doings are poorly thought out.
You should think about that, Gilgamesh.

"And you should think about the gods, Gilgamesh,
Who are always awake, awake and sleepless
While the moon and stars move across the sky,
And whose order is set from times of old.

How will you support them, Gilgamesh,
The temples of the gods and goddesses? *270*

"Yes, the gods bore Enkidu off to his doom.
You endured hard trials, but what did you get?
Exhaustion from all your grinding toil,
Your veins and sinews throbbing with grief,
Hastening your own doom, the end of your days.
A man's life is snapped off like a reed.
The handsome young man, the beautiful girl,
Death bears them away in the prime of life.
No one ever sees Death, the face of Death,
And no one has ever heard the voice of Death, *280*
Death who so savagely mows men down.
We found our households, build our abodes,
Brothers divide their inheritance,
Wars come and go across the land.
The river rises and brings us floods,
And floating on the water there is a mayfly.
The mayfly gazes on the face of the sun,
And then, in an instant, nothing is there.
A dead man is like one who is abducted,
But no one has ever drawn the face of Death, *290*
And the dead never greet anyone on earth.
The great gods, the Annunaki, met in assembly,
And Mammitu with them established destiny.
They established life and established Death,
But never do they reveal the day of Death."

TABLET XI

Utanapishtim and the Flood

Then Gilgamesh said to Utanapishtim
In that most distant land:

                  "When I look at you
Utanapishtim, you seem no different from me.
You are like me, and I am like you:
My heart was set on making you fight,
But now that I've met you, I stay my hand.
How did you meet with all the gods?
How did you gain eternal life?"

Utanapishtim answered Gilgamesh,

"I will reveal a mystery to you, Gilgamesh,   *10*
A secret of the gods. Shuruppak, the city
On the Euphrates' bank that you know well,
Was from ancient days dear to the gods.
The Great Ones were gathered there,
Their hearts set on sending down the Flood.
Their father, Anu, swore a great oath
Along with Enlil, their counselor,
And the court nobles Ninurta and Ennugi.
Ea too was there and swore with them,
Repeating their words to a wall made of reeds: *20*

72

'Wall of reeds, listen well, Wall.
Listen well, Reed-wall, Wall hear my words.
O man of Shuruppak, son of Ubar-Tutu,
Tear down your house and build a boat;
Abandon your wealth and strive for survival;
Spurn your possessions and cling to life!
Bring the seed of every living thing
Aboard the boat, aboard the ark you will build.
Build the ark square, length and width equal,
And roof it over as the Abyss is roofed.'   *30*

"I understood, and said to Ea, my lord,

'I understand, my lord, and will do as you say.
But what do I say to the city and the elders?'

"Ea opened his mouth and said to me, his servant,

'Say this to them:
                "Enlil hates me,
And so I cannot live in this city
Or look upon the land that is Enlil's.
I am off to the Abyss to live with Ea my lord,
And he will send you a plentiful rain
Full of birds and fish of all kinds,   *40*
An abundance of riches; in the morning
He will shower you with dark-baked bread,
And rain down wheat on you in the evening."

"When dawn first glimmered in the sky
The people assembled at Atrahasis' door,
Carpenters with their adzes, reed-workers,
Old men bringing ropes, boys carrying pitch.
By the fifth day I had the hull framed in,
One acre in area and ten rods high,
And the sides also were ten rods long.   *50*

Then I laid out the design for all the rest.
I put in six decks, which gave her seven levels,
And divided the interior into nine sections.
I put in bilge plugs amid-ship,
Got punting poles and rigged up the ropes.
I heated up thirty thousand measures of pitch
And loaded on thirty thousand measures of tar.
The porters brought thirty thousand measures of oil.
Not counting the ten thousand we used for libations.
There were twenty thousand stowed away on board.   *60*
I butchered oxen and lambs for my workers daily,
Served them rivers of beer and ale, oil and wine,
They feasted as if it were New Year festival days.
I started applying the oil at the break of day
And by sunset I had done the whole boat.
What came next was very hard work.
We rolled the boat down on logs, moving them
From back to front until she was two-thirds in water.
I loaded aboard everything I owned,
Loaded aboard all the silver I had,   *70*
Loaded aboard all of my gold,
Loaded aboard all the animals I kept.
I sent all of my relatives onto the ship,
Sent on beasts of the field and beasts of the wild,
And craftsmen and artisans of every kind.
Shamash had set for me a definite time:

'In the morning he will send you a shower
And in the evening he will send a heavy rain.
Go into your ship then and close the door.'

"The definite time arrived.   *80*
In the morning there was a shower
And in the evening a heavy rain.
I looked out to see what the weather was like,
And the weather was truly frightful to look at.

I went into the ship and closed the door.
I had left all my property to the shipwright,
To Puzur-Enlil, who now sealed the boat shut.
When dawn first began to brighten the sky
A dark, black cloud rose from the horizon,
And Adad the Storm God rumbled within it.   *90*
The gods Shullat and Hanish went before him
Shouldering the thunderhead that was his throne.
The god Errakal was uprooting the piers,
And Ninurta was busy overwhelming dams.
The Anunnaki lifted their blazing torches,
Spreading sheet lightning over all the land.
Adad passed over the sky like a shadow,
And all the brightness fell from the air.
He charged the land like a rampaging bull
And smashed it to pieces like a clay pot.   *100*
Gale-force winds blew for an entire day,
Blew hard as can be, and then down came the Deluge,
Sweeping like a battle over all the people.
A man could not make out a man before him,
No one could be recognized amid the havoc.
Even the gods were terrified of the Flood;
They fled up into the heaven of Anu
And lay there in the sky curled up like dogs.
Belet-ili cried out in her lovely voice,
Our Lady wailing like a woman in childbirth: *110*

'The days of old have turned into clay
Because I said bad things among the gods.
How could I say bad things among the gods,
Declare a war to destroy my people?
I am the one who gave birth to these people,
And now they fill the ocean like fish!'

"The Anunnaki wept along with her;
Tears in their eyes, the gods were weeping;

Their lips were dry and parched with fever.
Six days and seven nights the gale-winds blew, 120
The rain poured down, the Flood flattened the land.
But when the seventh day dawned
The winds died down, and the water subsided.
The sea that had writhed like a woman in labor
Now was calm, the storm over, the Deluge ended.
I opened a window, and sunlight fell on my face.
I looked at the weather, and it was perfectly calm,
But all of the people had turned into clay,
And the land was as flat as the roof of a house.
I sank to my knees and wept, 130
Tears running all down my face.
I scanned the ocean's horizon in all directions
And saw fourteen patches of land emerging.
The ship came to ground on Nimush Mountain,
Mount Nimush held it fast and did not let it move.
A first day and a second day Nimush Mountain
    held the boat fast and did not let it move.
A third day and a fourth day Nimush Mountain
    held the boat fast and did not let it move.
A fifth day and a sixth day Nimush Mountain 140
    held the boat fast and did not let it move.
When the seventh day dawned
I brought out a dove and let it go.
The dove flew off but then came back to me;
There was no place to land and so it came back.
I brought out a swallow and let it go.
The swallow flew off but then came back to me;
There was no place to land and so it came back.
I brought out a raven and let it go.
The raven flew off and saw the water subsiding. 150
It found food, cawed, and did not come back.
Then I sacrificed incense to the Four Winds,
Pouring out offerings on the mountain top.
I set out seven pots and another seven,

Piling beneath them cane, cedar, and myrtle.
The gods smelled the savor, smelled the sweet savor,
And gathered like flies around the sacrifice.
As soon as Belet-ili arrived, she lifted in prayer
The lapis lazuli beads Anu had made to court her:

'O gods, may the great beads in this necklace of mine,   *160*
Cause me to remember these days forever.
All of the gods will come to this sacrifice.
But to this sacrifice do not let Enlil come.
His mind was murky and he caused the Deluge,
Delivered my people to utter destruction.'

"As soon as Enlil arrived
He saw the boat and was filled with anger,
Raging against the Igigi, the gods:

'How did this creature get away with this?
No mortal man was meant to survive!'   *170*

"Ninurta opened his mouth and said to great Enlil:

'Who but Ea could make such a thing happen?
Only Ea understands these matters.'

"Ea opened his mouth and said to great Enlil:

'Great hero Enlil, wisest of the gods,
How could you so foolishly cause the Deluge?
Punish the criminal with his own crime!
Afflict the wrongdoer with his own wrong!
Loosen so it won't snap, tighten so it won't go slack.
Instead of bringing on the Deluge,   *180*
You could have sent a lion to thin out the people.
Instead of bringing on the Deluge,
You could have sent a wolf to thin out the people.

Instead of bringing on the Deluge,
A famine could have ravaged the land.
Instead of bringing on the Deluge,
The god of plague could have ravaged the land.
I did not myself reveal the great gods' secret.
I sent Atrahasis a vision and he learned it himself.
Now you must decide what to do with him.'   *190*

"Enlil came aboard the boat,
Took me by the hand and led me on deck,
Brought my wife on too and had her kneel beside me.
He stood between us, touched our brows and blessed us:

'Utanapishtim was a mortal man before,
But now he and his wife are like us, the gods.
He will dwell in the distance, where the rivers rise.'

"And they settled us in the distance, where the rivers rise.
As for you, who will call the gods to assembly
So you can come to have the life you are seeking?   *200*
Try going without sleep for six days, seven nights."

Gilgamesh had no sooner settled himself down
Than a fog of sleep drifted around him.
Utanapishtim said to his wife:

"Look at the man who so much wanted to live.
A fog of sleep has already drifted around him."

And his wife said to Utanapishtim the Distant:

"Touch the man and wake him up.
He will go back as he came, hale and hearty,
Back through the same gate and home to his land."   *210*

Utanapishtim answered his wife:

"Men are not honest. He will try to deceive you.
Bake for him daily a loaf of bread. Line them up
By his head, and mark the wall each day he sleeps."

So she baked loaves of bread daily, lined them up
By his head, and marked the wall each day he slept.
The first loaf of bread was completely stale,
The second was leathery, the third moldy,
The fourth loaf was turning white,
The color of the fifth was already gray,   *220*
The sixth loaf was freshly baked,
And the seventh loaf was still in the oven.

Then her husband touched Gilgamesh.
He awoke, and said to Utanapishtim the Distant:

"I had just drifted off to sleep
When you touched me and woke me up."

And Utanapishtim answered him:

"Gilgamesh, count for me your loaves of bread
And you will see how many days you slept.
The first loaf of bread was completely stale,   *230*
The second was leathery, the third moldy,
The fourth loaf was turning white,
The color of the fifth was already gray,
The sixth loaf was freshly baked,
And the seventh loaf was still in the oven,
And it was only then that I touched you."

Then Gilgamesh said to Utanapishtim the Distant:

"O Utanapishtim, what should I do, where should I go?
A thief has stolen my body.
Death has moved into my bedroom,   *240*
And wherever I go, Death will be with me."

Then Utanapishtim said to Urshanabi the boatman:

"May boat and dock disdain you Urshanabi.
Begone from this shore you once walked upon.
And as for the man that you brought here,
His body is matted with filthy hair,
And the pelts he wears have marred his beauty.
Take him to the bathtub, Urshanabi,
And let him wash his matted hair clean.
Let him throw his old pelts into the sea   *250*
And soak in the tub until his skin glows.
Have a new headband made for him to wear,
And royal robes that befit his dignity.
And until he comes home at last to his city
And reaches his journey's end, let his robes
Show no signs of wear, but stay clean and new."

Then Urshanabi led Gilgamesh to the bathtub,
And Gilgamesh washed his matted hair clean.
He threw his old pelts into the sea
And soaked in the tub until his skin glowed.   *260*
He had a new headband made for him to wear,
And royal robes that suited his dignity.
And until he came home at last to his city
And reached his journey's end, his robes
Showed no signs of wear, but stayed clean and new.

Gilgamesh and Urshanabi were the boat's crew.
They had launched it and were setting forth
When Utanapishtim's wife said to him:

"Gilgamesh toiled mightily to get here.
What have you given him for his journey home?"   *270*

Gilgamesh then picked up a punting-pole
And pushed the ship back up to the shore.
Utanapishtim then said to Gilgamesh:

"You toiled mightily to get here, Gilgamesh.
What can I give you for your journey home?
I will let you in on a secret, O Gilgamesh,
A deep secret, a mystery of the gods.
There is a plant that resembles boxthorn,
Very prickly to one who picks it,
But if you can come to obtain this plant   *280*
You will become a young man again."

When Gilgamesh heard what Utanapishtim told him,
He waded out to sea, clearing a channel,
Tied heavy stones to his feet, and the stones
Pulled him down to the Ocean's floor.
He found the plant there and plucked it out,
Cut the heavy stones loose from his feet,
And the sea carried him up and onto the shore.
Gilgamesh said to Urshanabi the boatman:

"This plant, Urshanabi, is the Heartbeat Plant.   *290*
It can restore to a man his youthful vigor.
I will take it to Uruk the Sheepfold
And feed some to an oldster to test it out.
Its new name will be Old Man Grows Young.
I will eat some myself and be young again."

At twenty leagues they stopped to break bread.
At thirty leagues they halted for the night.
Gilgamesh found a pool of cool water
And went in it to bathe. While he was there,
A snake caught scent of the aromatic plant,   *300*
Approached silently, and bore the plant off.
As it slithered away, the snake sloughed off its skin.
Gilgamesh sat on the ground and wept,
And as the tears coursed down his cheeks
He said to Urshanabi the boatman:

"For whom did I work so hard, Urshanabi,
For whom did I drain my heart dry of blood?
I didn't do anything good for myself,
Only did the earth-lion, the snake, a favor.
Now all along the shore the tide is rising.   310
When I opened the channel I left my tools behind.
What could I find to guide me to the spot?
I should have turned back, left the boat beached."

At twenty leagues they stopped to break bread.
At thirty leagues they halted for the night.
When they arrived at Uruk the Sheepfold
Gilgamesh said to Urshanabi the boatman:

"O Urshanabi, climb Uruk's walls and walk along them.
Examine the massive, terraced foundations.
Is the masonry not of fine, fired bricks?   320
Those foundations were laid by the Seven Sages.
One square mile is town, one square mile orchard,
One square mile clay-pits, and half a square mile
The temple of Ishtar. Three square miles and a half
Is the area of Uruk."

~ END ~

GLOSSARY OF DEITIES, PERSONS, AND PLACES

Adad: Storm God.

Annunaki: Group of the senior gods and goddesses of Mesopotamia.

Antu: Goddess of Heaven; wife of Anu.

Anu: God of Heaven; progenitor of the other gods and goddesses.

Aruru: One of the names of the Creator or Mother Goddess.

Atrahasis: "Exceedingly Wise"; earlier name for the survivor of the Flood, Utanapishtim.

Aya: Goddess of Dawn; wife of the Sun God Shamash.

Belet-ili: "Lady of the Gods," an epithet of the Creator or Mother Goddess.

Belet-seri: "Lady of the Wilderness"; divine scribe of the Underworld.

Bibbu: Divine butcher of the Underworld.

Bull of Heaven: Monstrous bovine in the charge of Anu; a manifestation of dangerous weather, including violent rainstorm and thunder as well as drought and resultant famine.

Cedar Forest: Timber-bearing region to the northwest of Babylonia, likely the Taurus or Amanus Mountains.

Dumuzi: Spirit of vegetal growth; spouse of Ishtar whom she had condemned to take her place in the Underworld.

Dumuzi-abzu: "Dumuzi of the Abyss"; aspect of Ishtar's husband in his Underworld exile.

Ea: God of Wisdom; champion of humans among the gods. Also called Enki.

Eanna: "House of Heaven"; temple of Inanna and Anu in Uruk.

Ebabbara: "House of Brightness"; temple of the Sun God in the city of Sippar, a town near Babylon.

Egalmah: "Exalted Palace"; temple of Ninsun in Uruk.

Enki: God of Wisdom; champion of humans among the gods. Also called Ea.

Enkidu: Primeval man who becomes the bosom friend of Gilgamesh.

Enlil: God of underground sweet waters; chief of the divine assembly.

Ereshkigal: Divine Queen of the Underworld.

Errakal: Epithet of Nergal, divine King of the Underworld.

Etana: Human hero who had flown to Heaven on the back of an eagle. Now deceased, he is an inhabitant of the Underworld.

Euphrates River: Western river of Mesopotamia; its northern reaches border the Cedar Forest.

Gilgamesh: King of Uruk, son of the goddess Ninsun and the mortal Lugalbanda, and therefore "Two parts god, one part human" (Tablet IX 43).

Hanish: Divine bull who along with Shullat pulls the chariot of the Storm God.

Humbaba: Monstrous guardian of the Cedar Forest, the nature of whose terrifying form is unclear. He was in the service of Enlil but was loathed by Shamash.

Hushbisha: A divine official of the Underworld.

Igigi: Group of the most important gods and goddesses of Mesopotamia, more or less equivalent to the Annunaki.

Inanna: Sumerian name of Ishtar.

Irnina: A name for the Underworld.

Ishtar: Semitic goddess of war and of sexuality; daughter of Anu.

Ishullanu: Human gardener of Anu; mistreated by Ishtar after he had rebuffed her sexual advances.

Larsa: City in southern Mesopotamia to the north of Uruk; one of the homes of the Sun God.

Lugalbanda: Human king of Uruk, divinized after death; father and patron deity of Gilgamesh.

Mammitu: One of the names of the Creator or Mother Goddess.

Marduk: The god of the city of Babylon. His mention in connection with the Cedar Forest is puzzling.

Mashu Mountains: "The Twins"; mythical mountains far to the east from which the Sun God rises in the morning.

Mount Lebanon: Mountain range in western Syro-Palestine.

Mount Nimush: Peak upon which the ark of Utanapishtim comes to rest after the abating of the Flood.

Mount Sirion: Mountain range in western Syro-Palestine, probably the Anti-Lebanon/Hermon chain.

Namtar: Personified "Fate"; messenger of death.

Ningishzida: "Lord of the True Tree"; divine chamberlain of the Underworld.

Ninshuluhhatumma: "Lady of Purification"; divine cleaning lady of the Underworld.

Ninsun: "Lady Cow"; divine mother of Gilgamesh.

Ninurta: God of war and conflict.

Nippur: City far to the northwest of Uruk; home of Enlil and early religious capital of southern Mesopotamia.

Nisaba: Goddess of grain.

Puzur-Enlil: "Secret of Enlil"; human carpenter who builds the ark for Utanapishtim.

Qassu-tabat: "His Hand Is Good"; divine janitor of the Underworld.

Scorpion People: Personages of mixed human–animal nature who guard the entrance to the tunnel leading to the ocean at the edge of the world.

Seven Sages: Semi-divine personages who conveyed the elements of civilization to humankind at the dawn of history; first builders of the city walls of Uruk.

Shakkan: God of grazing animals.

Shamash: Sun God; at home in both Larsa and Sippar.

Shamhat: "Harlot"; prostitute working in Uruk.

Shiduri: "Maiden" (Hurrian); tavern-keeper on the seashore at the edge of the world.

Shullat: Divine bull who along with Hanish pulls the chariot of the Storm God.

Shuruppak: City to the north of Uruk; home of Utanapishtim.

Silili: Divine mother of horses.

Sin: Moon God.

Stone Ones: Character uncertain—personages or things (?) whose presence was essential for the passage of the ferry of Urshanabi across the ocean at the edge of the world.

Sumuqan: Another name for Shakkan, god of grazing animals.

Thunderbird: Personified storm; a form of Ninurta.

Ubar-Tutu: "Friend of (the god) Tutu"; human father of Utanapishtim.

Ulay River: River to the east of Uruk in southwestern Iran. In Sumerian sources the Cedar Forest was thought to lie in the east, so Gilgamesh and Enkidu had followed its course on the way to confront Humbaba.

Urshanabi: Ferryman of Utanapishtim.

Uruk: City in southern Mesopotamia ruled by Gilgamesh.

Utanapishtim: "He Found Life"; man of Shuruppak, who along with his
     wife, are the sole survivors of the Deluge and are granted immortality
     by the gods. In the Old Babylonian tale of the Flood, he bears the name
     Atrahasis. As the only male human to have escaped death, Utanapishtim
     is the ancestor of all people, including Gilgamesh (Tablet IX 50).

SUGGESTIONS FOR
FURTHER READING

Abusch, T. 2015. *Male and Female in the Epic of Gilgamesh: Encounters, Literary History, and Interpretation.* Winona Lake, IN: Eisenbrauns. (Collection of essays largely approaching the Epic from a psychological perspective.)

Ackerman, S. 2012. *When Heroes Love: The Ambiguity of Eros in the Stories of Gilgamesh and David.* New York: Columbia University Press. (Consideration of the function of homosexuality in the tale of Gilgamesh and Enkidu and the Biblical account of David and Jonathan.)

Al-Rawi, F.N.H., and A. George. 2014. "Back to the Cedar Forest: The Beginning and End of Tablet V of the Standard Babylonian Epic of Gilgameš." *Journal of Cuneiform Studies* 66:69–90. (Recent additions to Tablet V.)

Beckman, G. 2018. *The Hittite Gilgamesh.* Atlanta: Lockwood Press. (Edition of the Gilgamesh material recovered at the Hittite capital with an introduction discussing the development of the textual tradition.)

Chen, Y. S. 2014. *The Primeval Flood Catastrophe: Origins and Early Development in Mesopotamian Traditions.* Oxford: Oxford University Press. (A thorough consideration of ancient Near Eastern narratives concerning the primeval Deluge.)

Damrosch, D. 2006. *The Buried Book: The Loss and Rediscovery of the Great Epic of Gilgamesh.* New York: Henry Holt. (Accessible account of the archaeologists and scholars whose efforts contributed to the recovery of the Epic.)

Finkel, I. 2014. *The Ark before Noah: Decoding the Story of the Flood.* New York: Nan A. Talese. (A British Museum Assyriologist's personal exploration of the development of the Deluge narrative in the Bible and the ancient Near East and the role of his predecessor George Smith in the recovery of the tale.)

George, A. R. 2003. *The Babylonian Gilgamesh Epic: Introduction, Critical Edition and Cuneiform Texts.* 2 vols. Oxford: Oxford University Press. (The standard modern edition of the Akkadian-language epic, probably too technical for most lay readers.)

Harris, R. 2000. *Gender and Aging in Mesopotamia: The Gilgamesh Epic and Other Ancient Literature*. Norman: University of Oklahoma Press. (Useful collection of essays by an Assyriologist on Mesopotamian literature.)

Heidel, A. 1963. *The Gilgamesh Epic and Old Testament Parallels*. Chicago: University of Chicago Press. (A comparison of the Epic with the Book of Genesis from a Christian confessional point of view; originally published in 1949.)

Kirk, G. S. 1970. *Myth: Its Meaning and Function in Ancient and Other Cultures*. Pp. 132–52. Berkeley and Los Angeles: University of California Press. (Analysis of the Epic in the context of a general study of mythical texts known from ancient and ethnographic sources.)

Lambert, W. G., and A. R. Millard. 1969. *Atra-Hasis: The Babylonian Story of the Flood*. Oxford: Clarendon Press. (Edition of the Old Babylonian text whose account of the Deluge was adapted for Tablet XI of the Epic.)

Maier, J., ed. 1997. *Gilgamesh: A Reader*. Wauconda, IL: Bolchazy-Carducci Publishers. (Collection of earlier essays on the Epic, many from difficult-to-access publications.)

Moran, W. L. 1995. "The Gilgamesh Epic: A Masterpiece from Ancient Mesopotamia." Pp. 2327–36 in *Civilizations of the Ancient Near East*, ed. J. M. Sasson et al. New York: Scribners. (Incisive consideration of the Epic by a master Assyriologist and sensitive reader.)

Steymans, H. U., ed. 2010. *Gilgamesh: Epic and Iconography*. Fribourg, Switzerland: Academic Press. (Collection of essays, most in English, on depictions of Gilgamesh in the art of the ancient Near East.)

Tigay, J. H. 1982. *The Evolution of the Gilgamesh Epic*. Philadelphia: University of Pennsylvania Press. (Study of the development of the Epic through the centuries in search of useful comparisons to the composition of the Hebrew Bible.)

West, M. L. 1997. *The East Face of Helicon: West Asiatic Elements in Greek Poetry and Myth*. Oxford: Clarendon Press. (Comprehensive discussion of the influence of Near Eastern traditions upon the literature of Classical Greece.)

Ziolkowski, T. 2011. *Gilgamesh among Us: Modern Encounters with the Ancient Epic*. Ithaca: Cornell University Press. (Survey of the influence of the Epic on modern creative writers.)

APPENDIX

Correspondences between Pages of This Edition and Lines of the Original Text

Page numbers of this edition (on the left) with corresponding line number ranges of the original text (on the right). Abbreviations here are as in Andrew George's 2003 edition. Tablet V includes material from Al-Rawi's and George's 2014 edition (itself abbreviated here as SB V 2014).

Tablet I
3	1–22
4	23–62
5	63–110
6	111–49
7	150–92
8	193–231
9	232–68
10	269–300

Tablet II
11	P 46–71, II 36–39
12	40–46, P 90–111, II 59–64, P 135–54
13	P 155–201, II 103–17, P 229–34
14	P 235–40, Y 18, II 162–91, Y 90
15	Y 97–19, II 216–33
16	234–41, Y 162–85
17	258–95
18	296–302

Tablet III
19	1–18
20	19–56
21	57–104
22	105–219
23	220–30, Y 272–87

Tablet IV
24	1–17
25	18–48

26   49–54, Bo2 12–24, IV 78–87
27   88–109, OB Ni 1–8, IV 20–21
28   122–41, OB Ni 9–19
29   OB Ni 20–26, IV 155–78
30   179–83, Ha1 3–7, IV 195–203
31   204–10, 239–60

Tablet V
32   SB V 2014 1–24
33   SB V 2014 25–72
34   SB V 2014 73–103
35   85–140
36   141–87
37   188–267
38   268–96, IM 27–29, V 300–303

Tablet VI
39   1–19
40   20–64
41   65–96
42   97–31
43   132–62
44   163–81

Tablet VII
45   1–30 (Hittite paraphrase)
46   31–33 (Hittite paraphrase), VII 37–68
47   29–103
48   104–45
49   146–76
50   177–208, 251–57
51   258–67

Tablet VIII
52   1–16
53   17–45
54   46–94
55   95–61
56   162–218

Tablet IX

Tablet X

Tablet XI